Jewish Elderly in the English-Speaking Countries

Jewish Elderly
in the
English-Speaking Countries

DAVID GUTTMANN

Bibliographies and Indexes in Gerontology, Number 10
ERDMAN B. PALMORE, SERIES ADVISER

GREENWOOD PRESS
New York • Westport, Connecticut • London

Library of Congress Cataloging-in-Publication Data

Guttmann, David.
  Jewish elderly in the English-speaking countries / David Guttmann.
    p. cm.—(Bibliographies and indexes in gerontology, ISSN
  0743-7560 ; no. 10)
  Includes indexes.
  ISBN 0-313-26240-3 (lib. bdg. : alk. paper)
  1. Jewish aged—Bibliography. 2. Jewish aged—Services for—
Bibliography. I. Title. II. Series.
Z7164.04G87 1989
[HQ1061]
016.3626—dc19   88-32347

British Library Cataloguing in Publication Data is available.

Library of Congress Catalog Card Number: 88-32347
ISBN: 0-313-26240-3
ISSN: 0743-7560

First published in 1989

Greenwood Press, Inc.
88 Post Road West, Westport, Connecticut 06881

Printed in the United States of America

The paper used in this book complies with the
Permanent Paper Standard issued by the National
Information Standards Organization (Z39.48-1984).

10 9 8 7 6 5 4 3 2 1

To my children, Ziv and Nirit—
with hopes for
their meaningful old age . . .

Contents

Series Foreword

The annotated bibliographies in the Bibliography and Indexes in Gerontology series provide insight to the question, "What is known in the field of gerontology?" Their purpose is simple, yet profound: to provide comprehensive reviews and references of the work done in various fields of gerontology. Since it is no longer possible for professionals to explore the vast body of research and writing in a subspecialty without years of work, annotated bibliographies are invaluable tools to the researcher.

This fact has become true only in recent years. When I was an undergraduate at Duke (Class of '52) I doubt anyone had even heard of gerontology. Almost no one was identified as a gerontologist. Now there are over 5,000 professional members of the Gerontological Society of America. When I was an undergraduate, there were no courses in gerontology. Now there are thousands of courses offered by most major (and many smaller) colleges and universities. When I was an undergraduate there was only one gerontological journal, the **Journal of Gerontology,** first published in 1945. Now there are over forty professional journals and several dozen books in gerontology published each year.

The reasons for the dramatic growth in gerontological interest are clear: the dramatic increase in the number of aged; the shift from family to public responsibility for the security and care of the elderly; the recognition of aging as a social problem; and, the growth of science in general. The explosive growth in knowledge in this field has resulted in the need for new solutions to the old problem of comprehending and "keeping up" with a field of knowledge. The old indexes and library card catalogues have become increasingly inadequate for the job, they are cumbersome and unwieldy to use, and keeping them current is an arduous task. On-line computer indexes and abstracts are one solution, but make no evaluative selections nor organize sources logically as is done here. Annotated bibliographies are also more widely available than on-line computer indexes.

These bibliographies are useful to researchers who need to know
what research has (or has not) been done in their field.   The
annotations contain enough information so the researcher usually
does not have to search out the original articles.   In the past,
review of literature has often been haphazard and rarely comprehensive because of the large investment of time (and money) that
would be required for a truly comprehensive review.   Now, using
these bibliographies, researchers can be more confident that they
are not missing important previous research, duplicating past
efforts, and reinventing the wheel.   It may well become standard
and expected practice for researchers to consult such bibliographies, even before they start their research.

The Jewish elderly are one of the most fascinating groups of
ethnic elders because of their rich variety of adaptations.   As
Dr. Guttmann states, "these people are perhaps the most culturally
heterogeneous among the aged populations anywhere. Their diverse
historical origins, disparate traditions, languages, and customs,
are sources of never ending fascination (or problems) for social
and behavioral scientists,...while their often conflicting approaches to health, health care, social welfare, and politics are
the basis for the existence of a wide variety of religious and
secular social and community services in each country and in each
major city."

This book is needed not only by academicians and researchers,
but also by the practitioners for educating and training personnel
to work with the aged, by Jewish communal services, and by informed Jews who want to better understand their elderly.

The author of this bibliography has done an outstanding job
of covering all the relevant information and organizing it into
easily accessible form.   Not only are there 283 annotated references organized into 6 chapters, but there is also an author index
and a comprehensive subject index with many cross-references for
the items in the bibliography.   Thus, one can look for relevant
materials in this volume in several ways: (1) look up a given
subject in the subject index; (2) look up a given author in the
author index; (3) turn to the section that covers the topic; or
(4) look over the annotations in Chapter 1 for basic knowledge and
general charateristics of Jewish aged.

In addition, there is a three page section on "Additional Resources on Jewish Aging and Aged," an eight page "Bibliography on
Aging in the Jewish World," and an eight page appendix of related
journals.

Dr. David Guttmann is an unusually qualified expert in the area of Jewish elderly because he has done so much research and writing in the field himself. He has also compiled other annotated bibliographies such as this one. His previous bibliography in this series, **European American Elderly (1987),** is already widely used. His annotations are concise and clear; one can easily understand the essence of the reference and therefore determine whether the original is worth pursuing.

So it is with great pleasure that we add this bibliography to our series. We believe you will find this volume to be the most useful, comprehensive, and easily accessible reference work in its field. I would appreciate any comments you may care to send me.

Erdman B. Palmore
Center for the Study of Aging and Human Development
Box 3003, Duke University Medical Center
Durham, NC 27710

Preface

Since 1654, when the first group of 23 Jewish immigrants arrived in New Amsterdam, Jewish migration to the United States has been nearly continuous. Today the Jewish population in this country is estimated to contain close to 6 million souls. According to the estimates of the JDC-Brookdale Institute of Gerontology and Adult Human Development in Jerusalem Israel which publishes statistics on the distribution of the Jewish people in the world by country and by major cities, of the close to 15 million Jews world-wide about 13 percent are 65 years old and older. Approximately more than one million Jewish elderly reside in English speaking countries--including Israel, and they are distributed in the following way: in the United States, 600,000; in Great Britain and in Ireland, 70,000; in South Africa, 30,000; in Australia and New Zealand, 14,000; and in Israel, 380,000. Thus the total estimated number of Jewish elderly in Englishspeaking countries is 1,094,000.

These people are culturally the most heterogeneous, perhaps, among the aged population anywhere. Their diverse historical origins, disparate traditions, languages, and customs, are sources of never ending fascination (or problems) for social and behavioral scientists, particularly for educators, historians, and anthropologists, while their often conflicting approaches to health, health care, social welfare, and politics are the basis for the existence of a wide variety of religious and secular social and community services in each country and in each major city. Despite this great diversity among the Jewish aged, there are several common elements that pertain to all of them at present and will exist in the future as well. There are still sizeable groups of elderly poor Jews in every major Jewish community. Long-term care, mental health, survivors of the Holocaust, the widows, the elderly without families, the chronically sick and disabled, and the dislocated pose special problems for the organized Jewish communities everywhere. Most Jewish communities foresee major communities everywhere. Most Jewish communities foresee major demographic changes that will influence the focus, the direction and the objectives of the planning bodies for services and the general welfare of Jewish aged in this and in the coming decades. These include an expected rise in the proportion of Jewish aged in the total Jewish population in each country; an increase of Jewish elderly in the "old-old" category (85+), requiring a much greater share of communal resources for their care either at home or in institutions; increase in higher education, especially in the "young" and "new old" (55 to 65 years old) age cohorts; and greater affluence for Jewish aged.

This annotated bibliography of published scientific works in the realm of social gerontology is the first and the most up-to-date work on this subject. It is the longest bibliography on Jewish elderly, encompassing 283 annotated entries and 113 not annotated publications that were published in the United States, Canada, Great Britain and Israel in the English language during the past fifteen years.

The reasons for compiling a separate book about the Jewish elderly are not difficult to state: researchers, policy makers, administrators, students and gerontologists need access to easily available and up-to-date information about what is known at present on this segment of the aged population; the practice world needs this knowledge as well for educating and for training personnel to work with the aged; Jewish communal services serving the aged need knowledge for their staffs about what is happening in the Jewish world, and especially about what is being developed, tested and used in serving the many faceted needs of the Jewish elderly; Jewish Federations and associated Jewish Charities, which provide the funding for the services, need to learn about the situation of Jewish aged, and about their satisfaction or dissatisfaction with the services they receive, in order to develop meaningful responses to the needs of the elderly in the Jewish community; cross-cultural sharing of knowledge enables us to learn from the experiences of other countries in reconciling the Biblical injunction of honoring the aged with the realities of the space age, and finally, interest in the situation and welfare of the Jewish aged within the "Jewish world" makes this bibliography a needed addition to the literature on aging.

This bibliography includes entries selected and assessed as to their relevance for the intended users. Each entry was annotated using two criteria:

1. The work refers with rare exceptions to Jewish aged in the gerontological sense, encompassing people who are 65 years old or older.

2. The work deals with studies, including doctoral dissertations, whose subjects are related to Jewish aged, or were conducted in Jewish agencies, institutions, and services.

The material is organized to help the reader identify the relevant information with ease, using either the chapter or part of the chapter that covers the topic, the subject index, the author index, or the list of journals and additional resources.

The methodology employed in securing available data about Jewish aged included a review of sources that were available through the computer, such as on-line searches of Social Work Research and Abstracts, The Social Sciences Citation Index, The Sociological and Psychological Abstracts, and the Dissertation Abstracts International. In addition, specific Jewish sources of publications not currently available by an on-line search were utilized.

The Structure of this Bibliography

The major concerns and issues affecting the welfare of Jewish aged, raised by community leaders, scholars, and practitioners in various forums constitute the heart of this work.

The first chapter provides the reader with some basic facts about the Jewish aged in many countries, their characteristics, customs, and traditions, and their cultural attitudes toward aging.

Chapter Two covers subjects that deal with immigration, settlement, out migration, and relocation of Jewish aged in the English-speaking world and in Israel. Studies that deal with political participation, and adjustment to the changed or changing social environments are included in this section of the bibliography.

The factors that are crucial for well-being in old age are
dealt with in Chapter Three. Personal and religious identity,
health, morale, income, employment, involvement in communal life,
and particularly family and community support, along with the
place and role of the religious institutions in support of Jewish
aged are presented.

Special problems affecting the well-being of Jewish aged,
whether in the area of mental health, widowhood, poverty, isolation, illness, crime, and many other social ills are presented
in Chapter Four. The ways in which older Jews cope with their
problems, and the responses of the organized Jewish communities to
their plights are highlighted. How people go about fulfilling
their filial responsibilities; how they struggle with often conflicting needs and interests of the generations; how they cope
with painful decisions about institutionalization of senile
parents and relatives are all documented.

Chapter Five addresses such issues as services delivery and
utilization by Jewish elderly. Outreach efforts by the Jewish
community to help the unaffiliated, special programs and projects
that are used in different parts of the world to alleviate the
plight of many isolated and/or lonely elderly are elaborated upon
to serve as models for services providers. Addressing the needs
of Jewish elderly can take different forms, such as provision of
direct services by Jewish agencies; financing the services that
are given by others; relying on the family, and/or relying on the
government for care of the aged. Each community has its own
unique way of using any one of these approaches alone or in some
combination. When the non-Jewish community assumes a major role
in services provision to all aged members of the society, Jewish
communities tend to shy away from this role. However, when the
services provided under non-sectarian auspices do not meet a
standard of service for Jewish aged that is considered important
by the professional and lay leaders of the Jewish community, there
is a tendency to supplement the services with the resources of the
Jewish community. Identification of concrete, emotional, and
spiritual needs are prerequisite for developing an informed plan
of intervention on behalf of Jewish elderly, while accessibility,
quality, and cost are key determinants in the use or non-use of
services by these people.

The last chapter includes articles and reports on education, training, and knowledge needed to work with Jewish elderly. Of special interest are studies that present the relevant values, and attitudes in working with Jewish aged in many different services. Group work, counseling, community organization, planning and advocacy are important elements of such work. Consequently, studies included in this chapter illustrate how these modalities and methods of work with Jewish aged can achieve their goals, and how these can apply to multi-ethnic groups of aged as well. Working with Jewish elderly requires education and training for attaining the knowledge and skills that are essential for meaningful interventions in the lives of these people. There are many subjects that may be beneficial to service providers and to students, such as cultural/religious heritage, traditions, attitudes to others, and beliefs. Focus on Jewish communal institutions, on the religious establishments, on the roles of Jewish federations, on Jewish social, cultural, educational, and health care agencies, and on models in education in services delivery enables one to comprehend the richness, the diversity. and the strength of these resources that need to be studied, understood and properly utilized in the provision of care for needy Jewish elderly.

There are additional rich resources for studying Jewish aging in most every major Jewish community in the English-speaking world, such as the local press, media, and audio-visual materials. These, however, were beyond the means of this author. Data presented in this bibliography speak for themselves. The interested reader can find not only what is currently known and available in social gerontological literature on Jewish aged, but, perhaps more importantly, what is missing, meagerly addressed, or in need of updating. It is hoped that the additional (not annotated) resources, and especially the listing of works, documents, and instruments secured through the courtesy of the JDC-Brookdale Institute of Gerontology and Adult Human Development in Jerusalem, Israel, will enrich, encourage, and enable the avid reader to seek innovations in methods and in services delivery and will lead to the creation of new services that will benefit, "new," "young," "old" and "old-old" Jewish aged, as well as the non-Jewish aged.

Acknowledgments

The compilation of this bibliography could not have been accomplished without the dedicated help of many individuals. I did this second book for the Series under the leadership of Professor Erdman B. Palmore, to whom I wish to express my sincere thanks and gratitude for his continued confidence in me. I appreciated the support and the encouragement of Professor Frederick L. Ahearn, Dean of The Catholic University's School of Social Service. Professor Robert L. Barker at the same school was particularly helpful to me with good suggestions for enriching the content of this bibliography and with his unselfish assistance in compiling the subject index.

The dedicated work of Mrs. Elnora McCree was already noted in my previous book. Here I wish once again to acknowledge her tremendous help with the typing and formatting of this book. Her assistants, Ms. Annette Newman, Mrs. Rose Queen, and Ms. Terri Miller are also commended for their untiring efforts in making this bibliography typing-error-proof...

Of the people who assisted me with the compilation of the relevant literature and initial typing, I wish to note with thanks Mrs. Hanita Ashury-Raphael, Mrs. Anat Froind and Mrs. Riva Friedman, at the University of Haifa, Israel, School of Social Work. To all of them I owe gratitude and heartfelt appreciation. Last, but not least, I wish to acknowledge the assistance of the JDC-Brookdale Institute of Aging and Adult Human Development in Jerusalem, Israel. My thanks for letting me use their list of publications on Jewish aging.

There were many others who provided assistance with a smile of encouragement, with a kind word, or with some challenging remarks, which helped to strenghten my resolve to complete this book as promised.

*Jewish Elderly
in the
English-Speaking Countries*

1 Characteristics of Jewish Aged

Demographic Information

1.   Bergman, S. (1980).   Israel.   In Palmore, E. B. (Ed.). International Handbook on Aging, Contemporary Developments and Research.   Westport, Connecticut: Greenwood Press.

This chapter presents three major trends in Israel: rapid aging of the population; increased awareness in society about the problems of the aging, and the corresponding need to allocate more resources for services to the aged, and the growing field of gerontology as area for practice, teaching, and research in higher education.   Demographic forecast until the end of this century needs to be translated into priorities in programs and services development.   There is also a need to develop manpower for long-term care.   Research and evaluation of services, and greater involvement of scientists in the welfare of the aged in Israel are advocated.

2.   Chenkin, A. (1984).   Jewish population in the United States, 1983.   American Jewish Yearbook.

Using the estimated number of households, and then multiplying this number by an average size of household figures, and discounting the number of non-Jews in these units, the estimated Jewish population in the United States in 1983 was a little under five and three quarter million persons.   While the largest proportion of Jews still resides in the Northeast and in the North Central states, there is a shift to the South and to the West, as in the general population of the country.   The distribution of the Jewish population by Regions, States, and by communities of 100 or more Jewish persons is presented in tables with helpful footnotes about the geographical definition of communities included in this survey.

3.   Fields, J. and Slater, W. (1985).   United States and Canada.
In Habib, J. (Ed.).   Survey of aging in the Jewish world: World-
wide report.   Papers on Aging in the Jewish World.   JDC-Brookdale
Institute of Gerontology and Adult Human Development, Jerusalem,
Israel.

Responses of 38 United States and 4 Canadian communities in the
worldwide survey of Jewish aged are cited and illustrated with the
aid of 25 tables.   Data are analyzed by city size as follows:
large: above 50,000; intermediate-large: between 15,000 and
49,000; intermediate-small: between 5,000 and 14,900, and small:
between 700 and 4,900.   Services provided by these communities are
presented.   Some services are provided on almost universal basis,
while with others there is considerable diversity.   City size has
a major effect on the range of services provided.   Generally
speaking, the larger the Jewish community the more services are
available to the aging.   Jewish sponsored services are used more
heavily than those offered under general auspices.   Both provision
and financing of services to the aged have increased over the past
five years.   Major demographic changes are foreseen in all communities, indicating growth for the elderly population, higher
educational levels than at present, and greater affluence.   Major
concerns cited in the large U. S. communities are: housing,
funding for services, and to a lesser degree, lack of manpower.

4.   Goldman, N. (1985).   Western Europe.   In Habib, J. (Ed.).
Survey of aging in the Jewish world: Worldwide report.   Papers on
Aging in the Jewish World.   JDC-Brookdale Institute of Gerontology
and Adult Human Development, Jerusalem, Israel.

This report contains data from Great Britain which is the only
English speaking country included in this part of the worldwide
survey.   There were 325,000 Jews living in this country at the
time the survey was conducted.   Close to one-fifth of this population are elderly: 64,000 or 19.7 percent.   Less than 4 percent
live in institutions.   None of the communities included report
contracting of new facilities.   Volunteer programs are universal.
Two-thirds of the communities offer various social and recreational programs and have old age homes.   Most services are available
to Jewish elderly regardless of their income levels.   There is a
need for planning services.   Differences in need for services
between the United States and Western European countries are
cited.

5.   Goldschmidt, N. (1985).   A brief guide to official statistics
on the elderly population of Israel.   Papers on Aging in the Jewish World, Draft for Comment. The JDC Brookdale Institute, Jerusalem, Israel.

Data on the size and characteristics of the aged population in
Israel are available from official sources that are referenced by
topic.   Censuses taken in 1972 and in 1983 resulted in special
publications on the aged.   These provide detailed accounts by demographic and socio-economic characteristics.   Data include information on labor force participation, family expenditure, health,
and use of health care services.   A number of specific surveys are
undertaken by various government agencies.   The Israeli Central
Bureau of Statistics published the results of the 1982- 1983 survey of persons aged 65 and over in households, excluding those in
institutions.   The survey was conducted with the assistance of a
number of public and government agencies.   The Bureau also prepares annual estimates of population by age groups, sex, country
of birth and marital status.

6.   Greenblatt, G. (1985).   South Africa.   In Habib, J. (Ed.).
Survey of aging in the Jewish world: Worldwide report.   Papers on
Aging in the Jewish World.   JDC-Brookdale Institute of Gerontology
and Adult Human Development, Jerusalem, Israel.

There are approximately 100,000 Jews in the four largest cities
of South Africa.   Close to one-third of the 68,000 Jews of Johan-
nesburg are elderly.   This community provides a wide range of
services to the aged, while the smaller communities have a much
more limited range and rely more heavily on government support.
Volunteer work and participation in Jewish voluntary organizations
are open to all elderly.   Development of housing services is plan-
ned in all four communities.   There is no organization for planning for the overall needs of the Jewish elderly in South Africa.
Lack of financial resources is seen as a main obstacle to the current and future development of services.

7.   Habib, J. (1985).   Survey of aging in the Jewish world:
Worldwide report.   Papers on Aging in the Jewish World.   JDC-
Brookdale Institute of Gerontology and Adult Human Development,
Jerusalem, Israel.

Representing the combined efforts of many persons, this survey
provides a most comprehensive and up-to-date picture about the
situation of Jewish aged in 79 participating communities worldwide.   The survey focuses on the challenges facing an aging society and on the ways in which these communities deal with the
needs of the elderly.   Critical issues reviewed include the role
of the Jewish community in provision of services to the elderly:
links between trends in general services and services for the

elderly, special issues in financing and programming, processes of planning and evaluation, and problems in meeting the needs of the elderly. Major findings are summarized for the entire survey population and detailed by countries, cities and continents. Innovative programs available in various communities are specified. These can stimulate replication and/or modifications elsewhere. A listing of 24 tables in the Appendix illustrate vividly the issues, needs and problems of Jewish aged as, well as the services and programs that Metropolitan Jewish communities have developed to deal with these.

8. Huberman, S. (1984). Growing old in Jewish America: A study of Jewish aged in Los Angeles. Journal of Jewish Communal Service. 60(4):314-323.

The elderly represents a larger proportion of the Jewish population than do the elderly of other ethnic and religious groups. In order to better plan for this group a more substantial data base is needed. The need to target services to those most at risk, the need for outreach, and specific program recommendations are elaborated.

9. Kop, Y. and Factor, H. (1985). Changing characteristics of the Israeli population and the utilization of health care services. Israel Journal of Medical Services, Vol. 21.

Between 1960 and 1980 the elderly population in Israel has grown threefold while the general population increased by only 70 percent. This dramatic growth in both absolute and relative numbers, has been a major factor in large increases in health care expenditures in Israel. Among the elderly 65 and over, the fastest growing age group is the 75 years old and older, who will place the largest demands on the Israeli health care system for hospitalization, physician visits, and rates of institutionalization. Widowhood among older women is another factor in their twice as high rate of institutionalization than among men.

10. Lippman, W. (1985). Australia. In Habib, J. (Ed.). Survey of aging in the Jewish world: Worldwide report. Papers on Aging in the Jewish World. JDC-Brookdale Institute of Gerontology and Adult Human Development, Jerusalem, Israel.

About one-fifth of the Jewish population in Australia's three main cities are elderly. All of these communities provide old age or nursing homes. Melbourne offers the widest range of services for its elderly. These include counseling, home help, day care,

social clubs, a sheltered workshop and a drop-in center. All communities encourage independence and good intergenerational relations. Most services are aimed at preventing premature institutionalization. There are no cutbacks foreseen in financing services for Jewish elderly. While all services are available
irrespective of income levels, all elderly and their families are
expected to contribute towards the cost of services. Each of the
three cities has a different problem in services provision, and
all need assistance with planning and evaluation.

11. Medoff, M. H. (1981). Note: Some differences between the
Jewish and general White male population in the United States.
Jewish Social Studies, 43(1):75-80.

Based on the 1971 National Jewish population study and compared
to the 1970 U.S. Census of Population for data on the general
white male population, this note shows that while 42.8 percent of
the Jewish males have at least a college degree - three times the
14.5 percent figure for the general white male population only
20.1 percent of Jewish males aged 65+ had similar educational
achievement. This discrepancy in education between the old and
the young generation of Jewish males is explained as the result of
different environmental and historic conditions. In the "Old
World" education was largely religious, while in the "New World"
it tends to be more secular. The majority of Jewish males aged
25 to 39 have graduated from college. Similar trends are noted
for employment, i.e. the older Jewish males had largely managerial
and administrative positions, whereas the younger generations, due
to their higher education, are employed mainly in white-collar oc-
cupations. These data differ significantly from the general white
male population, of whom only one-third are in managerial occu-
pations, while over one-half of them are in blue-collar and or
manufacturing work. These socioeconomic differences between the
two male populations are even more striking in their reported income levels, with Jewish households heavily skewed toward the
upper income categories.

12. Monk, A. (1987). The "new" and the "young" aged. The Journal of Aging and Judaism, 1(2):146-165.

The "new," the "well," and the "young" are new concepts in aging
that connote different meanings and relevance to the Jewish elderly. "Well" aged are people in their sixth and seventh decade of
life, free of serious impairments and able to seek new challenges.
Due to liberal perceptions of their capacities, a wider range of
activities are open to them to fulfill life-long dreams. Only 2
percent of persons aged 65 to 74 years require personal care
assistance in the United States, while 18 percent in the age
brackets of 85 years and older need such assistance. "New" aged
Jews are people in their mid-sixties who had experienced many
hardships, and who now want to enjoy a sense of security. The

"young" old constitute the "command" generation. These are people in their mid fifties to mid sixties who control all domains of public life. Since they possess good health, higher education, political power, and relatively high financial security, they seem to "have it all." Yet, they face the inevitable transition to old age and its consequences...

13. **Papo, M. A. (1984). Reflections on demographic studies of two communities. Journal of Jewish Communal Service,** 60(1):100–103.

Two demographic profiles based on studies of the St. Louis, Missouri, and Palo Alto, California communities highlight striking differences and similarities: a stagnant population growth, and a growing elderly population. These two studies raise important questions for policy makers with regard to funding of programs for senior services, which often conflicts with demands for funds for Jewish education services. Demographic studies offer "snapshots" of a single period in time. When several of them accumulate, one can see the trends that exist in a given community. Such studies are tools for education and for fund raising in addition to their traditional applications.

14. **Rosenwaike, I. (1987). A demographic profile of the elderly Jewish population in the United States in 1970. The Journal of Aging and Judaism,** 1(2):126–145.

Increased birth rates in the late 19th century and declines from these levels, especially during the period from 1930 to 1970, are seen as responsible for the steadily increasing proportions of the elderly in the Jewish population. Using the 1970 census for the Yiddish mother tongue populations, a portrait of the economic and socio-demographic characteristics of persons 65 years of age and over is drawn. The major segment of the elderly Jewish population still uses Yiddish in their daily communication. The 1970 census in which this proxy item was used to identify elderly Jews is considered representative of the elderly Jewish population. The majority of the Jewish elderly in 1970 were immigrants. Migration has contributed heavily to sex ratio differences. The ratios of married and widowed Jewish aged largely parallel those of the general population. Younger members of the Jewish aged (65 to 74 years) are mainly native born, are better educated and more affluent.

15. **Rosenwaike, I. (1974). Estimating Jewish population distribution in U.S. Metropolitan areas in 1970. Jewish Social Studies, 36(2): 106-117.**

Four Standard Metropolitan Statistical Areas were the sites for this study: Baltimore, Cleveland, St. Louis, and Washington. The purpose of the study was to identify the Jewish population and patterns of settlement. Use of the Yiddish language as mother tongue was found to be highly reliable in estimating Jewish population distribution in other cities.

16. **The demographic consequences of U.S. Jewish population trends. The American Jewish Year Book, 1983, 141-187.**

Demographic consequences of recent and future Jewish nuptuality, fertility, mixed marriages, and quantitative assessments of the dynamics of this population are reported in this article. The main data source cited as the basis for population projections is the 1970-1971 National Jewish Population Study, which has two important features: country-wide representativeness and a large sample size. Jews as a group are more aged than the entire white population of the United States. In the 65 years old and older age group, in 1980, there were 15.5 percent Jews as compared to 11.8 percent for all U.S. Whites. This age composition can be understood as largely resulting from changing fertility levels in the past. In 1980 the 65 and over were nearly as numerous as the children below age 15, and the potential exists for a further increase of the elderly in the near future as the age group of 50-64 was relatively large at that time.

17. **Thomas, K. and Wister, A. (1984). Living arrangements of older women: The ethnic dimension. Journal of Marriage and the Family, 46(6):301-311.**

Using data from the 1971 Canadian Census, this article examined the effect of cultural structures, measured by ethnicity, on the living arrangements of older, previously married women. These were singled out since fertility measures were available only for females, and since they were no longer in an intact marital relationship. Of the two dichotomies used in the analysis, the British/French and the Jewish/Italian, the latter is of particular interest. Jewish women displayed the highest rate of separate living. Fertility was found to be the major determinant of whether or not older women live alone. Ethnicity was another key variable in this respect, while socioeconomic characteristics and age had only some effect on living arrangements.

18. Tobin, G. A. (1985). Trends in Jewish demography and their effects on campaign planning. Journal of Jewish Communal Service, 62(1):139-146.

Jewish demographic studies cover the majority of the Jewish population in major cities of the United States. However, they tend to under-represent certain regions, such as the South, and the Southwest, and smaller cities as well. These demographics present the great diversity found within the Jewish communities by region and by service usage, and by patterns of fund raising and voluntarism. Jews seem to adopt, to as yet unknown degree, the cultural norms and behaviors of the cities in which they dwell. Differences due to location, economic conditions, status, organizational structure, and etc., are important variables that must be taken into consideration by planners of campaigns for fund raising. Jewish Federations are urged to seek such studies and to use them in their fund raising efforts, and for coordination of social planning among all communal services. New marketing techniques, new organizational models, and new institutions based on the changes found in the demography of the Jewish population as a whole in the past decade, and on projected population trends, are advocated.

Perspectives on Jewish Aging

19. Bergman, S. and Cibulski, O. (1981). Environment, culture, and adaptation in congregate facilities: Perspectives from Israel. The Gerontologist, 21(3):240-246.

Five selected studies from Israel which examine some aspect of adaptation of elderly persons to congregate facilities are reviewed. The highly diverse aging population of the country is dichotomized to Westernized-modern and to Oriental-traditional groups. These designations are considered important in understanding the aged's' background and familiarity with such facilities. Adaptation to the social environment is seen as a process whereby an organism accomodates to its environment, and is related to a person's happiness, morale and life satisfaction. Adaptation to the home is measured in two of the studies by five criteria: resident's feeling in the home; friendships formed; psychological well-being, outsider observer's index, and attendant evaluation index of adaptation. One of the outstanding findings in these studies is that those residents whose placement in the facility was on their own volition were perceived by the staff to be better adapted to the environment. The authors stress the need for more research on motivation to enter institutional care by the two major segments of the aged population in Israel.

20. Dresner, S. H. (1987).   Geriatric sex and the Jews.   The Journal of Aging and Judaism, 2(2):94-107.

This article is based on an exchange of letters between the author, a well known rabbi and scholar, and the chief officer of a metropolitan service agency for the aged. The issue discussed is whether or not residents of a Jewish Home for the Aged who are not married should be permitted in this place to engage in intimate relationships with each other. The article highlights the conflict between Jewish traditions and values, such as the sanctity of marriage, and modern attitudes to privacy in sexual matters. Rights of the residents to personal freedom and choice are juxtaposed with demands for the employment of an expert in Jewish values to maintain Jewish moral values and family traditions in this nursing home. The author claims that agency policies and regulations should reflect the Jewishness of the Home, and that the administrator should be responsible for the implementation of Jewish values there.

21. Frank, B. B. The American Orthodox Jewish housewife: A generational study in ethnic survival. Doctoral dissertation, The City University of New York, 1975. Dissertation Abstracts International, 36:5579-A.

American Orthodox Jews are a subgroup of the religiously observant Jewish population in the United States. These people manage to live in American culture by remaining firmly committed to their traditional religious way of life without turning away from the cultural patterns of the larger American society. Transmission of the orthodox heritage from one generation to the next by Jewish housewives is discussed as particularly interesting in contrast to the majority of Americanized Jews, who, in their process of assimilation, have discarded traditional Judaism.

22. Gelfand, D. E. and Olsen, J. K. (1979). Aging in the Jewish family and the Mormon family. In Gelfand, D. E. and Kutzik, A. J. (Eds.). Ethnicity and Aging, Theory, Research and Policy. New York: Springer Publishing Company, 206-221.

Using a historical analysis, the authors note that both of these two religio-ethnic groups have experienced persecution and hostility, and struggle to attain the desired upward mobility. They differ, however, in their outlook on the family, and in expectations from the family, for supporting the aged. For Mormons the family is the basic social organization in the Kingdom of God. Hence the emphasis on preserving the extended family. The Mormon Temple is a central factor in family life stability and in the lives of the elderly. Some older Mormons can carry out socially respected roles within the Church, such as missionary work, Temple work, or geneology. Older Jews, who are more assimilated in the

mainstream of life in American society, do not have similar roles
to play. The family in both of these groups experiences changes
with the resultant dimiuntion in its ability to provide expected
care for the needy elderly.

**23. Johnson, F. L. et al. (1984). Life satisfaction in the mi-
nority elderly. Issues in Mental Health Nursing, 6(1–2):189–207.**

Three groups of culturally and racially different elderly
Blacks, American Indians, and Jews aged 56 to 98 years old were
compared in a study to examine the influence of environmental factors on their life satisfaction. Using the Life Satisfaction Index - Form Z, the OARS Multidimensional Functional Assessment
Scale, and a measure of losses in old age, the authors found no
significant differences in the life satisfaction of these three
groups. Based on the findings, it is suggested that the distinc-
tive characteristics of members in minority groups be considered
in planning and in implementing nursing care.

**24. Kahana, B. and Kahana, E. (1985). Jewish aged and their
families: Cross–national perspectives. Papers on Aging in the
Jewish World. Draft for Comment, AJW–25–85. JDC–Brookdale
Institute of Gerontology and Adult Human Development, Jerusalem,
Israel.**

Recent trends in the Jewish family with implications on intergenerational relations are identified and analyzed. Available
data from diverse Jewish communities and from the main source,
namely research done in the United States, serve as resource material. Understanding the family relations of the diverse aged
population requires paying attention to the many changes in lifestyles and in social policy. The Jewish aged of today are different from their predecessors the authors state. There are methodological issues which need to be taken into consideration as
well. Comparability of data, for example, is one of those issues
that have relevance on the generalizability of conclusions drawn
from one study to another. Since Jewish families exhibit today
higher divorce rates, increased geographic mobility, greater labor
participation of women, and consequently less informal supports,
the aged have a greater need for communal supports. Meeting the
service needs of older family members requires a complementary
approach to caring between the family and the formal Jewish and
general services.

25. Kart, C. S. (1987). **Age and religious commitment in the American-Jewish community.** In Gelfand, D. E. and Barresi, C. M. (Eds.). Ethnic Dimensions of Aging. New York: Springer Publishing Co., 96-105.

The relationship between age and religious commitment in the American Jewish community is assessed. Traditional, life time stability, family life cycle, and the progressive disengagement models of church attendance are reviewed. Loss of religious commitment was a problem ever since the first Jewish immigrants arrived to America. Factors that affect the assimilation and the religious identification of American Jews are analyzed. Elderly Jews, the majority of whom came from Eastern-European communities, are disproportionately represented in the more traditional branches of Judaism. More than one-third of the members of Orthodox synagogues in America are 60 years of age and over. At present there is no clear cut empirical support for either the assimilationist view, which posits a continued decline across the generations, or for the stabilization view, which sees a halt among young Jews in the decline in religious observance. Gender differences in age and religious commitment need further study.

26. Kart, C. S., Palmer, N. M. and Flaschner, A. B. (1987). **Aging and religious commitment in a midwestern Jewish community.** Journal of Religion and Aging, 3(3/4):49-60.

The relationship between age and religiosity among American Jew was investigated. Religiosity was measured in two broad categories: organizational and individual commitment. Subjects were 286 "affiliated" Jewish heads of households, or his/her spouse, of whom close to three-fifths were female. Results indicate that among males the older the subject the more likely he will be holding multiple memberships in Jewish voluntary associations. Older females were found to be more religious, and more likely belonged to Jewish organizations than younger Jewish females. They also had very strong Jewish identities.
These results are discussed as to their generalizability to other Jewish communities. The need for further empirical testing of religious commitment is raised.

27. Katlin, F. (1982). **The impact of ethnicity.** Social Casework, 63(3):168-171.

Ethnic values affecting Jewish clients were blended with clinical social work in seminars for staff working in a Jewish agency with clients of similar religio-ethnic backgrounds. Participants shared memories, feelings, and experiences, and came to appreciate the importance of ethnic identity for both worker and client. Understanding the components of ethnic identity and of ethnic bonding are considered therapeutic tools for diagnosis and treatment.

28. Krause, C. A. (1982). Grandmothers, mothers and daughters: An oral history study of ethnicity, mental health, and continuity of three generations of Jewish, Italian, and Slavic-American women. American Jewish Committee, New York.

Offering a close look at three generations of ethnic women who live in the industrial Northeast, this study was undertaken to identify information about ethnic women and ethnicity as expressed and perceived by them that may be useful to educators, scholars and to professionals responsible for the delivery of mental health services. Retention of the ethnic identity is a central factor in the lives of these women. Despite some weakening of the informal supports, that traditionally were the major sources of good mental health, they are still extending their influence over the well-being of ethnic women. Identification of generational and ethnic differences in priorities, interests, and problems can help us recognize potential areas of conflict. It can also serve as a basis for the perception of common interests, values and goals, and may lead to coalition building for facing the challenges of modern society. These were the conclusions reached from this study of 225 women in Pittsburg equally divided among three generations of three major ethnic groups.

29. Pratt, N. F. (1978). Transitions in Judaism: The Jewish American woman through the 1930s. American Quarterly, 30(5):681-702.

A steady growth in the status of Jewish women was noted particularly in the 1920s and 1930s, when a number of Jewish women organizations have developed programs and activities in which women found opportunities for making significant contributions. Growth in status was predicated on economic factors and country of origin, that is eastern or western Europe, as well as on denominational affiliation. Differences between Reform, Conservative, Orthodox and Secular Jewish Women were evident in the attainment of social status, while the fear of assimilation into the Gentile culture acted as an inhibiting factor.

30. Reuben, S. C. (1987). Old age: Appearance and reality. The Journal of Aging and Judaism, 2(2):117-121.

Using the Bible as the source for a reflection on modern society's attitude towards the aged, the author ponders questions about old age, strength, decline, and appearance that shape the reality of Jewish approaches to aging. Long life is the reward for following God's commandments. The righteous enjoy not only wisdom, respect, and honor, but virility too. In Psalm 92 we read: "In old age they (the righteous) still produce fruit, they are full of sap and freshness" - like our Father Abraham. The

"spirit" of the age in which one lives determines a particular society's attitudes toward the old. One can share, or even transfer
today responsibility for the care of an impaired parent, unlike in
Biblical times. Yet, shunting off the aged parent to an institution usually results in feelings of guilt by the child. The need
for a sense of connectedness lies at the heart of the issue of how
to adequately deal with the problems of the aged and of those who
must be responsible for them.

31. Seltzer, S. (1983). Some Jewish perspectives on aging and
society. Generations, 8(1):28–30.

Judaism was never pollyannish in its treatment of aging, the author claims. The Old Testament presents its heroes in their old
age with all their frailties and weaknesses, while the prayer of
the Psalmist's plea of "cast me not off at the time of old age" is
a reminder to all of us of the fears of all aged. Longevity of
the Patriarchs and Matriarchs, while exaggerated, indicates that
life has possibilities that sometimes are best realized in old
age. They serve as lessons for the young. They provide models
for emulation and stress the need for intergenerational cooperation. The death of the Patriarch Jacob, as described in the
Bible, stands in sharp contrast to the loss of dignity suffered by
so many old people in society. Jacob dies knowing that his life
has been meaningful. How we prepare ourselves and our children
for the eventual exit from life can tell much about our attitude
to life.

32. Shanan, J. and Shahar, O. (1983). Cognitive and personality
functioning of Jewish Holocaust survivors during the mid–life
transition (46–65) in Israel. Archiv Fuer Psychologie, 135(4):
275–294.

Ninety subjects matched for sex, education, and national background were divided into three groups, two of them survivors of
the Holocaust and the third a group of Israeli inhabitants during
World War II, to study the long–term effects of exposure to prolonged massive stress. Subjects completed a battery of tests aimed at assessing differences in coping styles in the past and at
present. Contrary to predictions, survivors of the Holocaust were
more stable and more satisfied with their present situation than
the Israeli inhabitants, but their cognitive functioning was lower. These findings led the authors to the conclusion that the
patterns of adjustment exhibited by survivors of the Holocaust
resemble premature aging.

33. Simos, B. G. (1973).   Adult children and their aging parents. Social Work, 18(3):78-85.

A sample of fifty Jewish adult children reporting on sixty aging parents, who lived in the greater Los Angeles area, revealed that the children were intensively involved in helping their parents cope with a wide range of problems. Lack of recreational facilities and inadequate public transportation contributed to the isolation of many parents. The mere presence of the children when visiting was perceived by the elderly as emotionally supporting, even when there was little or no communication. These findings have implications for social work with all aged persons, for as professionals, social workers have to deal with physical, social and emotional needs and problems of the elderly.

34. Smolar, L. (1985).   Context and text: Realities and Jewish perspectives on the aged. Journal of Jewish Communal Service, 62 (1):1-7.

Using illustrations from the Old Testament, this article reviews Jewish traditions and perspectives on old age. It emphasizes the significance of care as an antidote to the elderly's fear of abandonment; how important it is that the aged stay among the younger generations as long as possible, and the impact of intergenerational relationships on the feeling of well being or abandonment of the old parent. The Jewish tradition sought over centuries to cushion the advent of the inevitable, to support the needy, and to urge the young to respect the old.

35. Stambler, M. (1982).   Jewish ethnicity and aging. Journal of Jewish Communal Service, 58(4):336-342.

Differences in attitudes among Jews toward aging are explained in terms of differences in degree of religiosity and religious affiliation. Orthodox Jews make better adjustment to aging than the non-orthodox due to their strong beliefs and faith in God, which helps them to overcome grief, loneliness and despair. Traditional ethnic and cultural values should be fused with modern ways of life. Specific features of the Jewish heritage, i.e. focus on the unity of time, and viewing old age as the stage for the full development of the reflective nature of man, are stressed.

36. Zeff, D. (1976). The Jewish aging: Problem dimensions, Jewish perspectives, and the unique role of the family agency. Journal of Jewish Communal Service, 53(1):81–87.

Jewish elderly are largely hidden and are not capable of militant advocacy on their behalf. They are also among the poorest, sickest, loneliest and fastest growing group in the Jewish population. Social planning committees should focus their attention on these people, while Jewish family agencies are requested to serve as advocates, helping them use to the full their government entitlements.

Jewish Traditions and Attitudes to Care of the Elderly

37. Gildin, N. B. (1985). Ethical and moral values in homes for the elderly. Journal of Jewish Communal Service, 62(2):178–180.

Ethical and moral values, their development, and adherence to their teachings, have been integral components of Jewish nationhood, history and ethnic heritage. These have bound together Jews, irrespective of their religious denominations over time, and have helped to maintain Jewish identity throughout the generations. At the Jewish Home for the Elderly of Fairfield County, Connecticut, a program pertaining to Jewish ethics has been introduced. Its purpose is to intellectually stimulate the "ethical nature" of the resident population. The program is conducted each week by the Home's Rabbi who uses an illustrated booklet in which each page denotes a different moral teaching and can be used for discussion in the weekly session. The booklet states that "this program is only a prologue to the Jewishness of our institutions in the future."

38. Gordon, N. A. (1975). The Jewish view of death: Guidelines for mourning. In Kubler–Ross, E. (Ed.). Death the Final Stage of Growth. Englewood Cliffs, New Jersey: Prentice Hall, 44–51.

The processes set forth in Jewish law and tradition provide a structure through which the loved ones of the dead person can mourn his loss and become reintegrated into the community of life. Beginning with arrangements for the funeral, continuing with the ritual tearing of the clothes, and with the shivah, or the seven days sitting in mourning, expressions of grief and sorrow are encouraged openly. The saying of prayer for the dead, the Kaddish, is a very important element and part of the grieving process that men and women should be allowed to participate in it. After the burial the focus shifts to the mourner. This is the time when the community reaches out to the mourner and begins the period of reintegration to life. In Judaism grief is organized throughout the year: the first three days for deep grief, followed by seven days of mourning, thirty days of gradual readjustment, and eleven months for remembrance and healing.

39. Hazan, H. (December, 1984).   Continuity and transformation among the aged: A study in the anthropology of time.   Current Anthropology, 25(5):567-578.

Temporal conceptions among the aged are explored by use of data from two anthropological studies in a day care center. The author argues that the constitution of the temporal universe is the cause of social behavior.   Clients of the day care center experience three consecutive modes of socially constructed temporality, of time sequencing, an attemporal "limbo" phase, and finally a pre-sent-bound temporal universe. The transition from a developmental perspective to a horizontal ordering of events represents a forma-tive period in the lives of the elderly.

40. Hazan, H. (1984).   Religion in an old-age home: Symbolic adaptation as a survival strategy. Ageing and Society, 4(2):137-156.

Religious activities can be used as strategies for survival. Data collected among 360 residents of an old-age home in Israel indicate that the symbolic manipulation of religious symbols can be observed at four levels of behavior: 1) among synagogue mem-bers and their study groups; 2) via the rabbi's lack of identi-fication with his congregation; 3) through the relationships of the residents with the nonreligious managers of the home, and 4) through the identification of residents who seem to function properly.
Religion is used by the residents as an important social re-source in their interactions with the nonresidents.

41. Hazan, H. (1980).   Continuity and change in a tea-cup: On the symbolic nature of tea-related behavior among the aged. Sociological Review, 28(3):497-516.

This study is based on ethnographic material collected during 1974-75 for a Ph.D. thesis. The author reviews the dialectics of continuity and change in the course of social transitions in later life.   The three convergent perspectives: macro-sociological analysis of cohorts and generations; role changes, and various theories of personality are not sufficient for understanding the complex phenomena of aging.   There is a need to study the inter-connection between a major transformation of social boundaries and the corresponding changes in a given set of symbolic behavior. The author performs this feat by discussing the act of tea-related behavior and its importance in a given culture, such as a day care center for Jewish aged in London.

42. **Heller, Z. I. (1975). The Jewish view of death: Guidelines for dying. In Kubler—Ross, E. (Ed.). Death the Final Stage of Growth. Englewood Cliffs, New Jersey: Prentice Hall, 38—43.**

The emergent concern with the welfare of the terminally ill is not new to Judaism. Tradition requires that the last stage of life be as anxiety free as possible. Death is confronted directly with specific view of terminal illness and dying as periods when loved ones should surround, comfort, and encourage the patient. The rituals of Jewish custom, set down in the "Shulchan Aruch" or the law, provide for dying in dignity. A dying person must set his house in order, bless his family, pass on any messages or directives, and make his peace with God. How meaningful are these requirements to the dying person depends on the Jewish identity of the individual, and on the integration of the Jewish values into the total way of life. The prescribed procedures accompanying the dying of the Jewish person, if followed with meaning, give an outlet to the needs of the dying person. The dying person is asked to repent, but the basic formula for repentance has a reassuring quality.

43. **Kaye, L. W. and Monk, A. (1987). Changing views of the function of the contemporary synagogue and the role of the older congregant. The Journal of Aging and Judaism, 2(1):4—18.**

The extent to which synagogues of the future be oriented toward the needs of the growing elderly population was investigated. Subjects were 142 students and 216 graduates from a major college of religious institution. These respondents were representative of four areas of specialized training in pastoral work: rabbinics, cantoral, educational and communal service. Findings confirmed that the students were confident in the capacity of the synagogue to provide a range of programs for the aged. Graduates, however, assigned greater importance to the educational functions of the synagogue. The two groups differed in perception of the roles and amount of participation of the older congregants in religious activities, as well as in their needs. While students thought that older people wanted mainly leadership positions, graduates with actual experience of working with the older congregants were convinced that the elderly are looking for spiritual support. From these findings the authors deduct that the next generation of rabbis can be expected to be more sensitive to the needs of the elderly congregants.

44. Linzer, N. (1986). The obligations of adult children to aged parents: A view from Jewish tradition. The Journal of Aging and Judaism, 1(1):34-48.

The moral obligations of adult children to support and nurture aged parents are explored from Judaic, ethical, and mental health perspectives. The primary filial obligations are to honor and to revere one's parents. Honor is expressed in acts, such as feeding, washing, covering, and etc., while reverence means refraining from behavior that might be cause for embarrassment to the parent. Each commandment has its own emotional state. Caring for the old is central to the ethos of the Jewish community. Children have to care for their parents as an expression of their gratitude for being born and nurtured by their parents. Financial obligations may at times conflict with the need to care for one's own children. Moral principles cited by the author are often at odds with Jewish traditional ideas of parenthood and allocation of support. There is a need for ethical sensitivity, and openness to ambiguity when dealing with moral complexities. The obligations of sons and daughters, caring for the mentally sick parent, and limitations on filial responsibility are elaborated.

45. Lomranz, J., Friedman, D. A., Gitter, G., Shmotkin, D. and Medini, G. (1985). The meaning of time-related concepts across the life-span: An Israeli sample. International Journal of Aging and Human Development, 21(2):87-107.

Six groups of Israelis, totalling 338 subjects and divided according to age, including 41 elderly in their sixties and seventies, participated in this study. The purpose was to rate five time-related concepts on the Semantic Differential Scales. Concepts rated were: time, past, present, and future. In addition, each group rated its own life stage. Findings point to significantly different perceptions of time-related concepts by age groups. "Past" ratings show a significant tendency to increase with progressive age, while "future" ratings decrease with progressive age. These and other findings are discussed in light of developmental processes and psychological adjustment. Further research with the Semantic Differential Scale is suggested in cross- sectional studies of time in the life cycle.

46. Mayer, E. (1977). Gaps between generations of Orthodox Jews in Boro Park, Brooklyn, N.Y.. Jewish Social Studies, 39(1-2):93-104.

Data derived from survey research, conducted in 1973 in a "living Orthodox Jewish community," are used to answer questions about the existence of the alleged generation gap between old and young. Interviews were conducted with 65 randomly selected families in

Boro Park in the homes of the respondents. A mailed questionnaire was also sent to 200 modern Orthodox youth group members of whom only 22 percent returned usable data. It was expected that this group would provide sources of intergenerational conflict due to the members modern and secularized lifestyles. Findings revealed that older respondents complained most frequently about the appearance of the young, their "radicalism" or liberalism toward sex and drugs, and interest of young Orthodox women in higher education and occupational careers outside of the family. Young people do not reject the basic underlyng values of their parents. Rather, they have different expressions of them, which at times conflict with those of the parents.

47. Meier, L. (1977). Filial responsibility to the senile parent: A Jewish approach. Journal of Psychology and Judaism, 2(1): 45–53.

Are children responsible for caring when their parents are senile? Jewish traditional teaching, anchored in the Talmud and in the work of Maimonides, is based on two concepts, kibbud, which in Hebrew means fear, and the avoidance of disrespectful acts. The child's responsibility is not altered when the parent behaves abnormally. Filial obligations still hold, but Maimonides made exceptions when the parent is mentally disturbed. In such cases the child is exempt from kibbud as personal service (but not from respect), while he is still responsible for arranging care for the parent by others.

48. North, A. J. and Ulatowska, H. K. (1979). Individual differences in cognitive functioning in the elderly—phenomena and interpretation. International Journal of Aging and Human Development, 10(4):359–371.

Twenty seven residents of a Jewish home for the aged comprised the study population. They were given a battery of tests to measure their cognitive abilities. Results indicated marked individual differences among the participants. Those who were diagnosed as having organic brain syndrome performed much poorer than others without this malady. Background variables were also associated with poorer performance among the subjects.

49. Pinsker, S. (1975). Piety as community: The Hasidic view. Social Research, 42(2):230–246.

The life, philosophy, and attitudes of Hasidic Jews in the United States is discussed, speculating on whether the traditional Jewish community is currently disintegrating.

**50.   Saul, J. M. (1983).   Jewish ethnic and psychological adjust-
ment in old age.   Doctoral dissertation.   Boston University Gradu-
ate School.   Dissertation Abstracts Internatinal, 44:1642-B.**

Forty subjects between the ages of 68 and 90 were interviewed.
The purpose was to learn about the role that ethnic identity plays
in aging. A variety of ethnic identity indicators were assessed,
among them subjects' self esteem, life satisfaction, and interview
behavior.   Findings revealed some significant relationships between ethnicity and psychological adjustment in old age. Ethnic
involvement in social activities was a critical factor in well-
being.   The role of the Jewish ethnic community in fostering
opportunities for sharing cultural and historical experiences is
discussed.

**51.   Shandler, M. A.   A study of the attitudes toward psycho-
therapy of American German Jews and selected groups of American
East European Jews.   Doctoral dissertation, The Catholic University of America, 1979.   Studies in Social Work, No. 131.   Dissertation Abstracts International, 40(2):1078-1079-A,   Order   No.
7918580.**

In this comparative study a sample of 60 German and 60 East
European adult Jews was interviewed.   Both groups are Ashkenazic
Jews, yet each group has a discrete identity.   German Jews are
known to have come from a more urban, affluent, entrepreneurial,
assimilationist, and religiously liberal background.   East European Jews, by contrast, came from a more rural, laboring, clan-
nish, and religiously orthodox background.   These characteristics
of the two groups were assumed to affect their attitudes toward
psychotherapy.
Findings indicated that the German Jews had statistically more
significant positive attitude toward psychotherapy than did the
East European Jews.   Prior experience with psychotherapy is independent of a person's background, Jewish identity, or religious
affiliation.   The author concludes that different ethnic groups
possess culturally determined attitudes toward social institutions
and services, and that these differ with each ethnic group.   Social workers are urged to incorporate such knowledge into their
services delivery system.

**52.   Shapero, S. M. (1987).   Gerontological narcosis.   The Journal
of Aging and Judaism, 1(2):87-95.**

This article is dedicated to the late Rabbi Maurice Eisendrath,
founder of the first formal gerontology program of the Reform Jewish Movement.   The author of this article served as director of
the Institute for Creative Development which has originated many
innovative programs for the aged.   Misconceptions about aging that
were prevalent in the sixties are discussed.   The need to awaken

from the gerontological narcosis by many religious institutions is cited. Organized Judaism, the author claims, is still lagging behind secular Jewish organizations and institutions in the development of a network of social services for the aged. There is a need to educate young people about the problems of the old and to stem the tide of resentment against them. The religious community should offer creative programs for the benefit of both young and old persons and to include courses in gerontology in their schools.

53. **Slotnick, D. (1987). Startled by faith. The Journal of Aging and Judaism**, 2(2):128–134.

Modern faith must be based on a clear vision of the world we live in, the author states. We must be able to detach ourselves as well as recognize our part in the community. There is a need to examine this three part prescription of detachment and vision leading to faith. This article describes the author's encounters with residents of a Jewish nursing home in New York City, and his attempts to teach himself and the residents that the acceptance of death does not betray the affirming of life.

54. **Spillman, D. M. (1985). Some practical considerations of the Jewish dietary laws. Journal of Nutrition for the Elderly,** 5(1): 47–51.

Kashrut are the dietary laws pertaining to food consumption by religious observant Jews. These laws were followed by the Jewish people from generation to generation since the giving of the Law thousands of years ago. The observance of these laws by elderly Jewish people forms a bridge with ancestors, children, the Jewish community and God, and often are associated with a sense of peace for the individual who has maintained this age old tradition. Caretakers of the elderly have special obligations to respect cultural traditions and to help clients observing these laws. A working knowledge of Kashrut is a must for dietitians who serve observant Jews.

55. **Spillman, D. M. (1985). Quick reference to favorite Jewish foods. Journal of Nutrition for the Elderly,** 5(1):57–64.

Many of the favorite Jewish dishes for elderly Jews are a combination of strict kosher laws and cultural heritages which stem from the countries in which these people once resided. Many of the terms used in these dishes are unfamiliar to young and/or non-Jewish professionals. To assist these people, a list of terms and dishes have been compiled by the author and organized into four food groups for easy reference: milk group, meat group, fruit and vegetable groups, and bread group.

56. **Vignola, S. L.** The American Jewish women's socialization process: The study of mother—daughter relationship as it affects the daughter's future choice of the husband. Doctoral dissertation, The Catholic University of America, 1979. Studies in Social Work, No. 129. <u>Dissertation Abstracts International</u>, 40(20): 1081-A. Order No. 7918583.

The associations between an American Jewish woman's early life experiences and her marriage to a Jewish or non-Jewish man, and such a woman's ethnic identity and continuity of Jewish ethnic values in the home she establishes, were studied with a sample of 72 women between the ages of twenty three and seventy one. These women volunteered to complete an anonymous, fixed-alternative, mailed questionnaire. A strong moderate correlation was found to exist between maternal Jewish identity, activity, warmth, and marriage to the Jewish or non-Jewish man.

2 Patterns of Settlement in the English Speaking World

Immigration and Residence

57. Grizzard, N. and Raisman, P. (1980). Inner city Jews in Leeds. **The Jewish Journal of Sociology,** 22(1):21-34.

The Jewish population in Britain has a reputation of having undergone a "successful immigration". However, there are still inner city Jews. This article describes one such inner city Jewish population in Chapeltown, Leeds. Once in the mid-thirties there was a thriving Jewish community of 20,000 in Leeds, of whom 12,000 lived in Chapeltown. By the end of the seventies, however, their number have fallen dramatically to about five hundred. More than three-fifths of the sample of 86 persons living in the 51 households surveyed were 65 years old and older, but if the "pre-elderly" of 55 to 64 years were included than the percentage would rise to 83.7. Thus inner city Jews in Leeds are old or aging, while there are no Jewish children under 15 in this neighborhood. These inner city Jews lead a rather segregated life from the larger Jewish community of Leeds, and lack a Jewish communal network for support.

58. Howe, I. (1976). World of our fathers, the journey of the East European Jews of America and the life they found and made. New York: Simon and Schuster, p. 714.

The monumental epic of Jewish immigration from Eastern Europe to America is told in this well researched and a well documented description of the great transformation in the lives of millions who for several decades, starting in the 1880's, undertook a massive immigration to the United States. A work of social and cultural history, tracing the fates of immigrants in New York City, but applicable to Jews of the same background who immigrated to other major cities, it is the story of the way they lived then; the restlessness of their learning, the culture of Yiddish, and the new life they established. Of particular interest are the chapters that treat the elderly, which depict generational conflicts

and the immigrant survivors, and provide valuable insights into
the soul and spirit of former and present day grandfathers and
grandmothers - remnants of a heroic age.

59. Huberman, S. (1984). Growing old in Jewish America: A study
of Jewish aged in Los Angeles. Journal of Jewish Communal Service, 60(4):314-323.

New immigrants, the poor, the sick, the very old, and people
with less than college education, tend to have the greatest need
for communal supports. Ironically, many of them do not use available social services. This article presents a demographic analysis of the elderly Jewish population in Los Angeles and advances
the idea of targeting services to those most at risk by both
social agencies and synagogues.

60. Jackman, J. C. (1979). Exiles in paradise: German emigres
in Southern California. Southern California Quarterly, 61(2):183-
205.

Hundreds of Jewish and non-Jewish Germans emigrated to southern
California during the 1930s and early 40s to escape Nazi Germany.
Among the refugees were such famous authors as Thomas Mann,
Bertholt Brecht, and Franz Werfel, who enjoyed continuing career
success. But other artists and intellectuals found it difficult
to adapt to the climate and life-style of southern California.
The biggest problem was adjustment to the changed conditions of
life. Employment was largely provided by the motion picture in-
dustry. For those who did not succeed, the European Film Fund,
organized by the celebrities among the exiles, provided aid.

61. Jacoby, S. (1979). World of our mothers: Immigrant women,
immigrant daughters. Present Tense, 6(3):48-51.

Jewish women immigrants are seldom discussed in the literature
on immigration. Especially lacking are accounts of their accomplishments and achievements in the United States. This article
discusses Jewish women immigrants to America since the late 19th
century. The conclusion reached is that traditional sex roles of
Jewish women of total devotion to family and socialization of
children are changing. The second generation immigrant daughters
are growing up with new, more modern, attitudes toward women's sex
roles. As a result they will be more able to transcend the accomplishments of their mothers.

62. Katan, J. and Stein, J. (1987). The elderly in an aging and shrinking Jewish community: Cape Town, South Africa. Journal of Jewish Communal Service, 63(4):321-328.

While the Jewish community in Cape Town is declining in number as well as in strength, the elderly population is growing. The need for comprehensive services for this group is discussed, pointing especially to the establishment of a community center for the provision of a wide range of cultural and social activities and services, including day care, along with a variety of medical, counseling, and transportation services. To expedite the development of services to the elderly, there must be cooperation among the various religious and communal organizations, as well as a willingness to coordinate both plans and resources.

63. Kesser, T. and Caroli, B. B. (1978). New immigrant women at work: Italians and Jews in New York City, 1880-1905. Journal of Ethnic Studies. 5(4):19-31.

This article is a historically based statistical analysis on the role of ethnicity in shaping the occupational distribution of women in New York City in the late nineteenth and early twentieth centuries. Italian women's upward mobility consisted of moving from initial unskilled to skilled blue-collar jobs. Jewish women, on the whole, generally started at higher status levels. Their progress was more rapid. Differences in attitudes to education and to family life were additional factors in the differential mobility patterns of Italian and Jewish women.

64. Kessner, T. The golden door: Immigrant mobility in New York City, 1880-1915. Doctoral dissertation, Columbia University, 1975. Dissertation Abstracts International, 36:3071-A.

Between 1880 and 1915 New York City attracted a very large number of immigrants. The newcomers differed from those others who preceded them because of their non-Protestant religion and their peasant folkways. These impoverished immigrants from south Italy and East Europe settled in New York's downtown neighborhoods. They also caused much concern among the nativists who feared that they would not be able to adjust to life in a big city. History proved these fears not particularly realistic, as Italians and Jews serve a good example of social mobility in America.

65. Krause, C. A. (1978). Urbanization without breakdown: Italian, Jewish, and Slavic immigrant women in Pittsburgh, 1900–1945. Journal of Urban History, 4(3):291–306.

Oral histories taken from immigrant Italian, Slavic, and Jewish women reveal their resiliency in meeting the cultural shock of immigration to the New World. These women used ethnic neighborhood organizations and their cultural bridges to the old world as bulwarks against mental breakdown. Their adjustment to life in America without a serious or lasting problem can serve as an example to present and future generations of immigrant women.

66. Kronick, R. F. (1987). Reported living preferences for elderly Jewish people living in Knoxville, Tennessee. The Journal of Aging and Judaism, 2(1):58–66.

Present living arrangements of elderly Jews living in Knox County, Tennessee were examined. Data were obtained by 23 students during the winter quarter of 1986. A total of 136 housing units comprised the study population. Of these, 53 persons completed the interview process. The purpose of the study was to learn about the living arrangement of Jewish aged and their future plans in this area. Findings revealed insufficient interest in creating a Jewish sponsored housing program for elderly Jews in this Southern city. Those who had plans for future living arrangements were more willing to be interviewed than those who did not have such plans.

67. Lewin, R. G.. Some new perspectives on the Jewish immigrant experience in Minneapolis: An experiment in oral history. Doctoral dissertation, University of Minnesota, 1978. Dissertation Abstracts International, 39:3778–A, Order No. 7823937.

Using 17 taped interviews with Jewish–Americans from eastern Europe, who came to the United States between 1900–1924, this study is a reexamination of stereotypes created by historians, social scientists, novelists, and film makers as to the immigrant experience. A social history of Minneapolis Jewry is attempted as well. The study emphasizes social process, individual behavior, and probable reasons for such behavior.

68. Lippman, W. and Borowski, A. (1985). Ageing in the Australian community. Papers on Aging in the Jewish World. Draft for Comment AJW-8-85. The JDC-Brookdale Institute, Jerusalem, Israel.

Demographic profile, needs, programs and services, and special problems of the Jewish aged in Australia are presented. At present, some 75,000 Jews are living in this continent. Ninety percent of this Jewish population are concentrated in two major cities (Melbourne and Sydney), and the rest are distributed in smaller communities. Aged Jews represent a larger proportion of the Jewish population than do the aged of the overall population. One quarter of the Jews in Australia are 60 years old and older and constitute one-third of the Jewish population of Queensland, which is considered the retirement state of the country. Social planning for the growing needs of the elderly by the organized Jewish community is done by the Jewish Social Service Council of Victoria. A common feature of all Jewish communities is the existence of Jewish Family and Child Service, or Jewish Welfare Societies. In the larger Jewish communities these services are highly professionalized, and they deal with the problems of the elderly. There is a need for research on the specific needs of the aged, especially on supports needed and available to them to maintain independent living in their familiar surroundings.

69. Shuval, J., Markus, E. J. and Dotan, J. (1975). Age patterns in the integration of Soviet immigrants in Israel. The Jewish Journal of Sociology, 17(1):151-163.

A sample of 1,566 immigrants from the Soviet Union to Israel was interviewed in 1971 to assess the relationship between age and adjustment over time to the new social system. The sample was stratified into four cohorts by date of arrival in Israel, with the average length of time of one, three, five, and ten years in the country. Major variables in the study included feeling and affect concerning the host society, solution of basic instrumental problems, and social integration. Findings indicated that the 65 years old and older started their stay in Israel rather euphorically, with higher morale than the younger immigrants, but their enthusiasm decreased over time. Length of residence in the country was not positively correlated with knowledge of Hebrew. Neither were their social interactions with neighbors and other Israelis. These findings were interpreted in light of the gerontological knowledge about the general losses and declines of old age.

Outmigration and Relocation

70. Frost, M. (1982).   Analysis of a Jewish community's out-migration.   Jewish Social Studies, 44(3-4):231-238.

Approximately 6,500 Jews in a midwestern United States city constituted the sample for a survey, conducted through the mail, to learn about their demographic characteristics. Of particular interest was the question whether or not these subjects follow the national trends and patterns for Jews, which include an increasingly aged population, high divorce rates, changing occupational structures, and an increasing intermarriage rate. Findings indicated an intention to move especially among the young. The impact of such move is theorized as being detrimental to the aged in age-segregated communities. A typology consisting of 6 types of residents is offered to increase theory development with respect to out-migration and as an aide to community planners and services providers to the elderly.

71. Goldstein, S. (1982).   Population movement and redistribution among American Jews.   The Jewish Journal of Sociology, 24(1):5-23.

Originally presented at the Eight World Congress of Jewish Studies in Jerusalem in 1981, this article reviews population movements and redistribution and their variability by region, age, sex, migration patterns and socioeconomic differentials. Of special interest is the finding that over three quarters of the married males have not changed their city of residence, while among older married women only five to seven percent had engaged in interstate movement in the five year interval. The impact of mobility on Jewish identity, and on the increasing degree of assimiliation, including intermarriage is stressed.

72. Kahana, E., Kahana B., Segall, M., Riley, K. P. and Vosmik, J. L. (1986).   Motivators, resources and barriers in voluntary international migration of the elderly: The case of Israel-bound aged.   Journal of Cross-Cultural Gerontology, 1(2):191-208.

Situational factors that differentiate successful from unsuccessful planners of voluntary long distance moves among the elderly were developed and tested on 162 potential migrants to Israel. Analysis of the results revealed that attachments, personal ties and familiarity with the new environment were significant predictors of moving. Movers were differentiated from nonmovers by their selective evaluation of the advantages of the new environment and by their assessment of the obstacles that stand in their move. Good health and being married were additional resources in facilitating the move to a new country.

73. Prager, E. H. (1986).   Elderly movers to Israel. Journal of Cross-Cultural Gerontology, 1(1):91-102.

A sample of 223 English-speaking relocators to Israel was surveyed at a one-day conference dealing with life in Israel. Investigation of the relationship between types of activity participation, and post-relocation adjustment and morale was the focus of this effort.   Only involvement in formal activities, such as active participation in organizations, philanthropic voluntary activities, and/or civic and political movements, were found to be significantly correlated with an index of adjustment. Participation in informal, high intimacy, or solitary activities was found to have no significant effect on indicators of adjustment/morale. Long distance relocation necessitates the forging of new relationships between the self and the environment.   Formal, task-centered areas of activity constitute sources of involvement and provide an arena in which continuity between present and past concepts of self may be facilitated.

74. Prager, E. H. (1985).   Older English-speaking immigrants in Israel: Observations on their perceived adjustment. Journal of Jewish Communal Service, 61(3):209-218.

The voluntary relocation of the aged to another country has received scant attention by gerontologists, especially the immigration to Israel by English speaking elderly Jews from the U.S., Canada, Great Britain, Australia, and South Africa. This article reports on, and discusses, the meaning of data collected from 223 older English-speaking relocators to Israel.   The majority of these relocated because of ideological reasons, not out of family considerations. Many were active in Jewish organizational life in their countries of origin, especially in America. While the majority of these immigrants felt rather integrated into Israeli society, and have found a "niche" or corner to live more or less comfortably, many need assistance, especially counseling to cope with the hardships of the transition to a new culture.

75. Rosenwaike, I. (1986).   The American Jewish elderly in transition. Journal of Jewish Communal Service, 62(4):283-291.

Between 1970 and 1980 an increase of 3.5 percent has occurred in the proportion of the Jewish aged within the total American Jewish population. While the latter increased vary slightly in number, the growth of the elderly during this decade was at least 29 percent. The graying of the Jewish population in America is noted with concern. At the present Jewish elderly (65 years and over) are estimated to be 15.5 percent of the total American Jewish population and 12.2 percent of all whites. This difference is largely due to a low level of fertility among Jewish women. Available data indicate that the future cohorts of Jewish aged will be very different from the present one. This difference is attributed to being born and raised in America, to being better educated, to being more concentrated in the four largest cities in the U.S. and to a gradual decline in the use of the Yiddish language. Greater visibility of the Jewish aged will also mean greater demand for services.

76. Simos, B. G. and Kohls, M. (1975). Migration, relocation and intergenerational relations: Jews of Quito, Ecuador. Gerontologist, 15(3):206-211.

A study of Jewish young adults reporting on their 60 to 88 year old parents was carried out among the Jewish refugees in Quito, Ecuador, with the aid of a semi-structured questionnaire. Findings revealed long standing personality problems and family discord as sources of intergenerational strife. Important subcultural group variations in life styles need to be studied for planning of adequate services, as life styles of country of origin persevere despite geographic relocation. The losses of aging can be mitigated by adequate personal and community resources and by family respect and closeness. Successful coping with the new environment requires access to educational and economic opportunities in the larger society.

77. Ucko-Greenbaum, L. (1986). Perceptions of aging East and West: Soviet refugees see two worlds. Journal of Cross-Cultural Gerontology, 1:411-428.

Perceptions of government policies, pensions, old age homes, family responsibilities and public and private attitudes toward the elderly were studied. Subjects included three-generation Soviet refugee families settled in the United States and in Israel who left the Soviet Union during the 1970s to join relatives in those two countries. They were questioned to gain information on aging in the Soviet Union. Comparison of these three societies' attitudes to aging, as per the respondents, indicates that in the Soviet Union there is much personal respect and family care, while government programs are seen as unreliable and inadequate. Old age homes in that country were especially criticized by these refugees. The situation in the West (i.e. in Israel and the United States) was perceived in reverse, that is praise for government programs, especially for higher social security and pension payments, and for the lack of stigma for receiving government benefits, and severe criticism of personal and family attitudes and care. The impact of thse perceptions on adjustment of these refugees to their new social environments is explored.

78. Weinfeld, M. (1980).   The Jews of Quebec: Perceived anti-semitism, segregation, and emigration.   The Jewish Journal of Sociology, 22(1):5-20.

The Jews of Montreal constitute almost the entire Jewish popula-tion of Quebec (98 percent).   They have deep roots in Canada. Close to one-third of them (31 percent) are over 65 years.   In this exploratory study, the relationship between perceived anti-semitism Jewish communal segregation and between propensity to emigrate was examined.   An elaborate data collection methodology was used to identify Jewish households — from which a sample of 657 completed questionnaires were obtained.

After providing an interesting historical background of Quebec Jews, the author presents his major findings.   These include a propensity to emigrate should Quebec become an independent state, due to perceived antisemitism felt by half of the sample.   Age had little effect on this perception.   Major trends revealed in this study point to more social than economic segregation among Jews in Montreal.   The author stresses the need for further study of both economic and social segregation, and the need for a redefinition of antisemitism to conform with the new macro-sociological empha-sis in its expression.

3 The Well-Being of Jewish Elderly

Preservation of Ethnic/Religious Identity

79. Averbach, J. S. (1976). From rags to robes: The legal profession, social mobility, and the American Jewish experience. American Jewish Historical Quarterly, 65(2):249-284.

The experiences of Jewish lawyers and their struggle for recognition and success in the legal profession are reviewed from 1900 to the present. Marred by prejudice and ostracism on the part of the elite, who preferred to exclude Jews from the benches, many Jewish lawyers became not only prominent on Wall Street but attained national recognition, culminating in serving on the Supreme Court. Jewish lawyers are prominant in the civil rights organizations, and are among the staunchest defenders of professionalism in the practice of law in the United States.

80. Chumaceiro, R. M. (1982). Language maintenance and shift among Jerusalem Sephardim. International Journal of the Sociology of Language, 37:25-39.

A sociolinguistic study was conducted in 1971 about the use of Spanyol, or Ladino, among Sephardic Jews in Jerusalem, Israel. Subjects were 28 men divided into young and old groups by age. The neighborhood of Yamin Moshe was selected as the site for the study. This neighborhood was practically homogeneously Sephardic before the 1948 War of Independence in Israel. It was assumed that inhabitants of this neighborhood were exposed to the Spanyol language for decades as their mother tongue. Therefore it was interesting to find out who still speaks Spanyol among the informants. Findings revealed a smooth transition to the Hebrew language and to opposition to teaching Spanyol in Israeli public schools. Lack of interest in transmitting this language and the Sephardic tradition to the younger generations is analyzed.

81. Citron, H. and Kartman, L. L. (1982). Preserving sexual
identity in the institutionalized aged through activities. Activities, Adaptation and Aging, 3(1):55–63.

The importance of sexual identity, and activities that help in
reinforcing, preserving and enhancing its quality in a nursing
home environment, is discussed. Through various activities, such
as belly dancing, which is described in greater detail, sexual
energy can be channeled into means of expression as socially
accepted outlets. Men's and women's clubs, music groups, and
dancing, for both sex-segregated and mixed-gender activities, contribute to the overall sense of well-being among the residents,
when these are encouraged in a caring and a warm nursing home
environment.

82. Costa, M.   Effects of sex and social affiliation on self-
attitudes and attitudes towards peers of an aging Jewish population.   Doctoral dissertation, Rutgers University, The State
University of New Jersey, 1979. Dissertation Abstracts International, 40:5388–5389–B.

A total of seventy five elderly participants in a congregate
luncheon program served as the sample in a study designed to learn
about aged individuals' relationships between self-attitudes and
aging. Results supported the idea that a person who is self-
accepting will be accepting of others. The results also suggested
that affiliation may be an important factor in self-attitudes.
Cultural factors and the appropriateness of the measuring devices
are analyzed as to their possible influence on these findings, and
the need for further research is discussed.

83. Dulin, R. Z. (Fall–Winter, 1986).   Elderly in biblical society. Journal of Aging and Judaism, 1(1):49–56.

The Bible presents varied opinions and thoughts concerning old
age. Biblical writers portrayed aging in a realistic and a pragmatic way and were cognizant of the physical and the psychological
changes that accompany the aging process. Old age was viewed as
the final phase of the developmental process, the last and most
difficult stage of human experience, but also a time of strength
and beauty. Old people played active roles in society, but not
all received support from their families. The pragmatic view of
life contained in the Bible is applicable to modern society, particularly the obligation to care for the aged and to refrain from
following a more expedient path.

84. Ginsberg, Y. (1981). Jewish attitudes toward Black neighbors in Boston and London. Ethnicity, 8(2):206-218.

Interviews with 100 elderly Jews from Boston and with 50 from London revealed a similar attitude toward Black neighbors in racially mixed neighborhoods. While subjects distinguished between "good" and "bad" Blacks, they were generally fearful and perceived Blacks as aggresssive, violent, loud, lazy, and dirty. They also tended to blame blacks for the high crime rate in the city. The similarity of perception and attitudes is interesting considering the fact that the London Jews had Black neighbors of much lower socio-economic status than those in Boston. Since contact with neighbors alone cannot explain the similarity of attitudes, other factors such as cultural heritage may be operating.

85. Gitelman, P. J. Morale, self-concept, and social integration: A comparative study of Black and Jewish aged, urban poor. Doctoral dissertation, Rutgers University, The State University of New Jersey, 1976. Dissertation Abstracts International, 37(6-A): 3907-3908.

Racial, ethnic, and religious differences, although significant, are not sufficient in and of themselves to account for aging individuals' self-appraisal and morale. Two distinct groups of aged urban poor Blacks and Jews formed the study population. Adjustment to old age was measured by three dependent variables, each subdivided into four dimensions: morale, self-concept and social integration. Married Blacks generally scored high on all dimensions, as anticipated, while married Jewish females scored the lowest. Findings confirmed the impact of religion, race and ethnicity on adjustment to old age. Implications for policy planning and service delivery are presented along with ideas for future research.

86. Hazan, H. (1983). Discontinuity and identity: A case study of social reintegration among the aged. Research on Aging, 5(4): 473-489.

This article is a different version of the study cited among the elderly Jewish residents of a poor neighborhood in London, England. Observations on their behavior in a day care center seem to illustrate how the discontinuance of past ties and involvements can aid them in the construction of their new identity. Identity formation in old age is more the function of new environmental and personal factors than continuity of previously established lifestyles.

87. Hazan, H. (1982). Beyond disengagement: A case study of segregation of the aged. Human Organization, 41(4):355-359.

A one year anthropological study of a day care center for elderly Jewish residents of a poor neighborhood in London, England, served as basis for several important observations. Chief among them the one which states that structural disengagement can lead to a state of reengagement in an age-segregated setting. Older residents countered feelings of alienation and near total social isolation with an alternative social reality, in which fraternity, equality, and personal autonomy were the reigning characteristics of behavior in the day care center. The hypothesis which states that the aged are capable of significant behavioral changes in later life is amply supported by the findings of this study.

88. Holzberg, C. S. (1983-1984). Anthropology, life histories, and the aged: The Toronto Baycrest Centre. International Journal of Aging and Human Development, 18(4):255-275.

"From Our Lives," the Baycrest Terrace Memoirs Group in Oakville, Ontario (published by the Mosaic Press in 1979) is the culmination of a project that began informally to keep a group of elderly Jews socially engaged. The Canadian government provided financial support for the publication of this book of memoirs to encourage replication of similar projects among other groups of elderly persons. The value of writing memoirs for the individual, the group and the community is described on the basis of personal experience by this noted anthropologist.

89. Jacobovitz, I. (1988). Ethical guidelines for an aging Jewish world. The Journal of Aging and Judaism, 2(3):145-157.

Jewish teachings regarding the attitude towards the aged are cited to critic treatment of the aged, communal budgeting for their needs and mitigating the problems associated with the tide of aging in the Jewish world. There is a need to restore the place of honor and the high esteem for the aged contained in Jewish Biblical and rabbinical sources to solve some of the problems of the aged, the author claims. To achieve this aim there should be: (1) an extension of the working age of men and women; (2) encouragement of life-long learning and education; (3) to fully reintegration of the elderly into the family, so that they will not require special protection of legislation or the support of communal care; (4) safeguarding their independence and dignity; (5) providing communally sponsored hospices, and (6) raising a new generation of teachers, social workers, children and parents suffused with the above values.

90. Moore, D. D. The emergence of ethnicity: New York's Jews, 1920–1940. Doctoral dissertation, Columbia University, 1975. Dissertation Abstracts International, 36(12–A):8255.

Children of the immigrants, or the second generation, raised the question of the nature of group assimilation into American society rather vividly.   Acculturation, accompanied by ethnic group persistence, was the answer. In New York City between 1920 and 1940 second generation Jews accommodated themselves to American life while they fashioned social and cultural institutions to promote Jewish ethnic group separateness.

91. Siegel, M. K. A Jewish aging experience: A description of the role of religion in response to physical dysfunction in a sample of Jewish women 65 to 83. Doctoral dissertation, Harvard University, 1976. Dissertation Abstracts International, 38(2–A): 722.

Variation in the experience of physical aging among a group of 33 women aged 65 to 83 within a Jewish subculture was explored. The response of these women to the aging process is described as generally positive. Religion provides an avenue for compensatory values and viable female roles in advanced age for the losses experienced by physical aging. Health is a major value either as an end in itself or as a means to some other goal. Time-based terms such as "eternity" are used to reveal patterns of experience with aging and to secure a sense of identity consistent with the Jewish tradition and heritage. Yet, time is perceived also as the source of crisis, potential, and requirement.

92. Weisman, C. (1985). The needs of the Jewish elderly: What's happened to spirituality? Papers on Aging in the Jewish World. Draft for Comment AJW–16–85. The JDC–Brookdale Institute, Jerusalem, Israel.

Statistics about the growth of the U.S. and the Jewish elderly population are presented. Implications of this growth are illustrated with a discussion on long term care. Following these backgrounds, the author focuses on the spiritual needs of elderly Jews. Jewish literary, religious, and philosophical sources are used to define spirituality which is seen as transcending nature, or that aspect which lies beyond one's comprehension. It draws on inner resources, and is primarily concerned with thoughts and feelings. Questions raised by the elderly center on a quest for self-understanding. They are expressions of the search for spirituality. Coming to terms with one's age, making peace with self, accepting one's responsibility for things that happened in

his or her life, and recognizing the significance of one's contributions to others are all part of this quest. Spirituality nour-
ishes one's identity, helps one to develop wisdom, and creates
opportunities for inner growth.

93. **Zimmerman, M.** (1987). **Toward Kol Nashim.** The Journal of
Aging and Judaism, 2(2):112-116.

The oral history of the author's grandmother and her striving
for Jewish identity serve as basis for the need to include female
insights into all aspects of Jewish life - including those that
pertain to the aging. Biblical female heroes are cited as examples to emphasize the point that women bring new understanding
to Jewish theology. Their creative contributions in applying
Judaism to our contemporary lives need to be recognized.

Factors Influencing Well-Being Among Jewish Aged

94. **Andron, S.** (1985). **Understanding Jewish community needs:**
The Greater Los Angeles regional needs survey. Journal of Jewish
Communal Service, 61(2):126-137.

Needs assessment research is a valuable tool in program development, as it lends itself to a variety of approaches in the continuing examination of the relevance of existing services to the
changing needs of aging. This article presents one such approach
utilized by the Jewish Federation Council of Greater Los Angeles.
In this survey, a total of 237 individuals took part. Findings
reported pertain to this group. Among the most serious problems
found with respect to the aging were isolation, lack of institutional care, no elderly home help, and lack of affordable elderly
housing in the community. The lists of social and communal problems offered in the appendix are useful for creative approaches
to future needs assessment surveys.

95. **Berrol, S. C.** (1976). **School days on the old east side:** The
Italian and Jewish experience. New York History, 57(2):201-213.

Many of the present generation of elderly Italian and Jewish
Americans grew up on the east side of New York City. Their school
day experiences in the early decades of the 1900's are compared.
These immigrants from the Old World brought with them their traditional attitudes toward education which explain the differences
between the two ethnic groups with respect to academic success.
Jewish children in general were taught by their parents to look
upon education as the key to success, while Italians were more
leery of the school's place in reaching the same goal. Only in
later generations, with the growing Americanization of the Italians, were the academic performances of these two groups more
equal.

96. Brunn, L. C. (March, 1985). Elderly parent and dependent adult child. Social Casework, 66(3):131-138.

The Jewish Family and Children's agency of Philadelphia and its services for older persons has developed a clinical approach for dealing with the complex problems of aging. Clients, from sixty five to eighty years old, ask for help in providing for the future care and protection of their dependent adult children, whose continued dependency on the aged parent is attributed to retardation, mental illness, and physical disability. The agency's help for these parents has been a direct result of the deinstitutionalization movement of the community mental health system. Caseworkers dealing with these populations need to utilize theories of adult development and aging and to view the problems of dependency in light of family functioning and relationships.

Life-cycle issues of old-age, and invisible loyalties among members of a family affect the feeling, thinking and motivations of each person. These, in turn, provide rich material for group and individual oriented casework. Formation of support groups, and focus on practical and emotional issues facing such clients are recommended.

97. Chetkow-Yanoov, B. (1986). Leadership among the aged: A study of engagement among third-age professionals in Israel. Ageing and Society, 6(1):55-74.

Differences between leaders and non-leaders, and variables which may account for them were explored. Subjects included members of the helping, the creative, and the public service professions, who had worked at least twenty five years. Data were gathered by means of mailed questionnaires. Findings indicated that the largest percentage of leaders emerged from the public services professions who also had the most optimistic outlook on life. Many of the respondents fit into more than one type of leadership. Characteristics of those defined as "high leaders" were also identified. Leadership enhances the professionals' lives in retirement.

98. Eden, D. and Jacobson, D. (1976). Propensity to retire among older executives. Journal of Vocational Behavior, 8(2):145-154.

This study of 179 top executives aged 55 years old and older in 13 leading Israeli organizations sought to determine favorable attitudes toward retirement. Findings indicated that feelings about oneself was more closely associated with positive attitude toward retirement than features of the job. Preference for continuing working was not a factor of age, but a feeling of health and effectiveness among these older executives. Types of withdrawal from the job and retirement, their similarities and differences are discussed.

99. Getzel, G. S. (1985).   Intergenerational reminiscence in groups of the frail elderly. Journal of Jewish Communal Services, 59(4):318-325.

Reminiscence in old age is discussed as occuring between and within generations. A conceptual framework for understanding the meaning of intergenerational themes in reminiscence is presented. Reminiscence groups offer potential benefits to old people, such as aiding them to solve current problems, an opportunity to review their lives, and to gain mastery by fulfilling the teaching function with respect to the education of the younger generation. Case illustrations are presented to describe the work of the professional worker with a reminiscence group in a day hospital of a large geriatric center. Five themes common in such work are raised and discussed along with the demands they pose for the worker. Working through the resistance of group members is a central concern, but peer support allows the elderly to explore deeply felt problems.

100. Getzel, G. S. (1980).   Old people, poetry, and groups. Journal of Gerontological Social Work, 3(1):77-85.

Forming poetry groups and writing poetry by old people have their problems and potentials. The author lists four obstacles that must be overcome by the leader/writer who works with the aged in such groups. These are: 1) the persistent and largely unavowed doubt that the aged can write poems in the group; 2) the writer's confrontation with a group member's hopelessness; 3) the reluctance of the writer to acknowledge the sources of pain and tragedy in poetry and in group discussion, and 4) the writer's giftedness, his knowledge, and his intuition. Collaborative and individual writing assignments, as well as readings and objects of beauty could be used by the writer to encourage old people to take on risks in revealing themselves through poetry writing. Writing groups are pleasurable experiences for old people. They provide opportunities for reflections on life and its meaning, and to sharing feelings and experiences by group members.

101. Golander, H. and Hirschfeld, M. (1981).   Nursing care of the aged in Israel. Journal of Gerontological Nursing, 7(1):677-680.

This article reviews the history of health care and nursing services to the aged in Israel. The rapid rate of increase in the number of aged is attributed to three factors: prolonged life expectancy due to favorable living conditions and availability of modern health care services; low birth rate among the Jewish population, and high percentages of old and middle aged immigrants.

Today's aged in Israel are almost all foreign born, and seventy percent of the aged immigrated at age 50 or later. Demand for nursing services for the aged is on the rise. Due to visible demographic changes in the "graying of Israel," the health care needs of the aged are given more recognition by policy makers and by professionals. A number of programs were developed by various agencies, but lack of coordination and overlapping of services are still common. Gerontological nursing is being gradually integrated into the basic formal education of nurses in Israel through a network of continuing education programs. In recent years some research projects were devoted to studying nursing personnel in geriatric institutions.

102. Golant, S. M. (1984). Factors influencing the locational context of old people's activities. Research on Aging, 6(4):528–548.

Data obtained from a sample of 400 persons aged 60+ and living in a middle class urban community, to identify where they usually pursued 13 different activities, indicate that those who tend to pursue their activities outside the proximate residential environment are likely white, Jewish, reasonable healthy and in possession of cars, or availability of other flexible means of transportation. These results are discussed in terms of their implications for interpreting the voluntariness of activity patterns among the elderly.

103. Greenberg, N. S. and Rosin, A. J. (1982). Factors influencing admission or nonadmission of the aged to the hospital. Journal of the American Geriatrics Society, 30(10):635–641.

Factors influencing actual admissions to a general hospital in Israel were studied. The purpose was to distinguish characteristics of patients admitted to the geriatric ward of the medical division from those sent to the internal medicine ward. The sample included 200 patients aged 65 years and over of whom 35% were not admitted. The rest of the sample was almost evenly divided between those admitted to internal medicine and those who were sent to the geriatric department. Acuteness and severity of illness were key factors in the selection process. Geriatric patients were functionally more severly impaired than the rest of the sample. They also had higher mortality rates and a higher degree of disability on discharge from the hospital.

104. Guttmann, D. (1984). Logophilosophy for Israeli retirees in the helping professions. International Forum for Logotherapy, 7 (1):18-25.

Retirement lifestyles of older Israeli helping professionals were investigated utilizing three theoretical approaches to aging. Subjects were 136 physicians, nurses, and social workers living in retirement for various lengths of time. Findings support the continuity theory for adaptation to old age. Israeli helping professionals at present can be characterized as largely "maintainers," that is, people whose involvement in professional activities in their own professions continues while in retirement. Of the three groups of health care professionals, only the social workers have shown some tendency toward new ventures in life outside of their profession. Implications of the findings for the use of leisure time and for preparation to retire are presented.

105. Harel, Z. and Noelker, L. (1982). Social integration, health and choice. Research on Aging, 4(1):97-11.

This study in 14 nursing homes and homes for the aged in the Cleveland metropolitan area examined the relative importance of the residents' social integration, along with health, socioeconomic status, and attitudes toward entry and residence on their subjective well-being. Findings revealed that the residents relied primarily on their children, family members, and friends as their primary sources of help, social contact, and emotional closeness. Fellow residents and staff were relied on by less than 10% of the residents. Self-rated health, and functional status were additional determinants in feelings of well-being. Implications of these findings for policy and practice with institutionalized aged are presented.

106. Kremer, Y. (1985). Parenthood and marital role performance among retired workers: Comparison between pre- and post- retirement period. Ageing and Society. 5(4):449-459.

Data collected from 310 former industrial and service workers were examined within the context of family functioning after retirement. Israeli parent, grandparent, and marital role activities after retirement were compared with the retrospective evaluation of the pre-retirement period, with the assumption that there will be a change in the daily schedule due to large amounts of free time, which the husband and wife could spend together, and use to improve their marital role and parental role investments.

Findings of the study indicate the difficulties inherent in dif-
ferentiating between parental and grandparental roles. Financial
assistance to the children was rather common. There was no decline in parental and marital functioning. The finding also
indicate that elderly parents are able to reciprocate assistance,
perhaps due to their economic security, and to maintain satis-
factory levels of sharing and communications with their spouses.

**107. Kremer, Y. (1984-1985). Predictors of retirement satisfac-
tion: A path model. International Journal of Aging and Human
Development, 20(2):113-121.**

The adjustment of 310 former industrial and service workers in
Israel to retirement was studied using path analysis. The respondents indicated a general sense of coming to terms with the loss
of work and enjoyed a more relaxed lifestyle. The retirees' evaluation of giving up work, activities with family and friends, rest
and tranquility, and free time were the dominant variables in this
path model, while situational, and behavioral variables, except
for educational level and subjective state of health, had negligible effects on overall satisfaction with retirement.

**108. Kremer, Y. and Harpaz, I. (1982). Leisure patterns among re-
tired workers: Spillover or compensatory trends? Journal of
Vocational Behavior, Vol. 21, 183-195.**

Retired industrial and service workers in three industrial
plants, representing the three main employing sectors in Israel -
the government, the private and the labor union - were selected
for studying the effects of retirement upon leisure behavior patterns among former employees. Subjects were 310 male retirees who
have been retired for 1 to 3 1/2 years. Data were examined within
the context of spillover and compensatory hypotheses, with
retirement representing the nonwork sphere.
The compensatory hypothesis suggests that workers who experience
deprivation at work will compensate for the deficiency by becoming
involved in nonwork activities which are more gratifying. Findings of this study point to no change in leisure behavior patterns
among these retirees in both pre and post retirement activities.
Thus the compensatory hypothesis is rejected. Findings also reveal a high degree of passive and solitary leisure behavior pattern which remains consistent from working life to retirement,
thus lending support to the spillover model for this group of
retirees.

109. Linzer, N. (1987).   Cross-currents in aging: Public policy
and the Jewish response. The Journal of Aging and Judaism, 2(2):
78-83.

Ethical impact of the shift from attention to the patient's personal needs to cost containment is discussed vis-a-vis the government institution of DRG as the policy for medical reimbursement to
hospitals. Levy's classification of values, originally conceived
to understand the nature and diversity of professional values that
guide actions, is used to distinguish between the societal and the
Jewish value structures in relation to the aged. The value base
of the DRG policy is cost containment. Therefore patients can be
discharged prematurely, regardless of whether they have conva-
lesced from the illness that brought them into the hospital. In
contrast to this policy, Jewish tradition has a preferred concep-
tion or value of the aged. They are seen as repositories of wisdom. Old people have dignity and capacity for decision-making in
all matters that apply to their health and well being. Professional workers should therefore involve them in important decisions concerning their lives. Since the DRG policy is seen as
ethically wrong, Jewish professionals are urged to take various
actions to protest against policies that demean the sick aged.

110. Novich, L. (1985).   Meeting the needs of the Jewish elderly
in Canada: Executive summary.   Papers on Aging in the Jewish
World.   Draft for comment AJW-4-85, The JDC Brookdale Institute,
Jerusalem, Israel.

The needs of the Canadian Jewish elderly and the means by which
they are met are summarized. Close to 93 percent of all Canadian
Jews reside in nine cities, of which Toronto and Montreal represent approximately three-quarters. While the aged 65+ comprise
9.5 percent of the country's population, Jewish aged 65+ represent
15.8 percent of a total Canadian Jewish population of 312,000.
Canada has an excellent medical care service which is available to
all aged, including the Jewish elderly. Long term institutional
care is available to Jewish aged in Jewish institutions in the major cities, but in small communities aged Jews must enter non-Jewish nursing homes and may be deprived of their religious needs.
Poverty among Jewish aged is decreasing due largely to government
programs on behalf of all aged. Day hospitals and low cost housing, transportation and facilities to serve the frail non-institu-
tionalized elderly are among the most important unmet needs. A
taxi subsidy program in the Winnipeg Jewish community is cited as
a practical solution to the transportation needs of Jewish aged
that should be emulated by other communities.

4 Special Problems of Jewish Aged

Aging of the Holocaust Survivor

111. Assael, M. and Givon, M. (1984). The aging process in Holocaust survivors in Israel. American Journal of Social Psychiatry,
4(1):32–36.

Effects of the Holocaust and subsequent forced immigration on
the aging process were studied. Subjects included 39 Holocaust
survivors, 30 newcomers to Israel, and 3 native born elderly.
These 72 Israeli psychiatric patients, 60 years old and older,
were compared as to their characteristics of physical illness and
mental disorders. Holocaust survivors among the subjects experienced more complicated symptoms, and more severe psychological
problems, than did their peers in this study. They also had poorer prognosis. Implications of these findings on the aging process
of older people who underwent severe psychological traumata are
presented.

112. Berezin, M. A. (1981). The aging survivor of the Holocaust
Introduction. Journal of Geriatric Psychiatry, 14(2):131–133.

Aging survivors of the Holocaust were the subject of a scientific meeting of the Boston Society for Gerontologic Psychiatry, held
November 22, 1980, with the author serving as the moderator. Out
of this meeting came a number of articles gathered in this volume.
Each generation must learn and know this piece of history, the author states, for as Santayana has said, "Those who cannot remember
the past are condemned to repeat it." Those who study the Holocaust are like the oncologists of society, and they face a painful
and a difficult exercise. For oncology is that branch of medicine
that is devoted to the study and management of malignant tumors.
The Holocaust was perhaps the greatest malignancy in history. It
has to be studied and understood in order to apply to it all the
curative and prophylactic measures and prevent its recurrence.

The characteristics of the aging survivor, and the impact of the experience on him and her were the specific subjects discussed at this meeting. Psychodynamic theory based on psychoanalysis served as the framework within which most of the presentations were made.

113. **Cath, S. H. (1981). The aging survivor of the Holocaust, discussion; the effects of the Holocaust on life-cycle experiences: The creation and recreation of families.** Journal of Geriatric Psychiatry, 14(2):155-163.

Human capacity to adapt and survive even the greatest of horrors is so vast that we can only touch on understanding it, the author states. The works of Dr. Ornstein and Sylvia Rothchild are cited as illuminating in this respect in particular. We are all survivors in some respect. Those who lived through the horrors of World War II experienced to greatly varying degrees the traumas caused by the war. Personal experiences with a survivor helped the author gain a better understanding of self. This survivor's love of life, despite all his sufferings, gave hope that feelings are not forever numbed in the survivors. Many survivors restitute for their missing offsprings and grandchildren by "adopting" a family in the neighborhood in which they live. This "parenting" often constitutes the first miracle in the long and painful process of their revitalization.

114. **Danieli, Y. (1981). The aging survivor of the Holocaust, discussion: On the achievement of integration in aging survivors of the Nazi Holocaust.** Journal of Geriatric Psychiatry, 14(2): 191-210.

This discussion begins with a review of the major concepts culled from the work and observations of Dr. Krystal on survivors of the Holocaust. Four tasks are identified as essential for survivors to achieve integration: the need to remember, despite the pain in bringing up memories; the need to "accept" what has happened in their past; the need to take a psychological risk to fight against "walling-off" the pent-up emotions, and the need for mourning and grieving. Discussions with aged survivors and empirical evidences are cited to validate Krystal's approach to the psychology of the aged survivor. Difficulties related to functioning by aged survivors are related to their shrinked or nonexistent support system, to role reversals between parent and children who both are survivors, and to the children's inability to care for the aged parent in such families. The conclusion reached is that aged survivors are unable to accomplish integration with their diminished capacities for the task.

115. Harel, Z., Kahana, B. and Kahana, E. (1977). The effects of the Holocaust: Psychiatric, behavioral, and survivor perspectives. Journal of Sociology and Social Welfare, 915–933.

Most of the research done on survivors of the Holocaust had several theoretical and methodological limitations. Theoretically, the research draws heavily on psychoanalytic concepts, neglecting in the process behavioral and social science perspectives. Inferences drawn from the data often go beyond the scope of the studies. Since the mid–seventies some efforts were made by researchers to bring behavioral and social science perspectives to bear on this area of research. These are perceived by the authors as useful for developing an understanding of the long-range effects of the Holocaust on survivors.

116. Herzog, J. M. (1981). The aging survivor of the Holocaust, Father Hurt and Father Hunger: The effect of a survivor father's waning years on his son. Journal of Geriatric Psychiatry, 14(2): 211–223.

Effects of the Holocaust on children of the survivors are a growing area of scientific and social activity. Study groups formed in major U.S. cities seek to discover whether such children tend to develop certain specific qualities by virtue of their parents' experience. The author focuses on one man's experience with his aging survivor father and on the way in which both therapist and son tried to understand the impact of those waning years in the life of the survivor on his son. This son was referred to treatment due to feelings of depression, trouble in relationships with women, and lack of spontaneity. Issues in transference are raised and discussed and the resolution of the conflict and traumatic relationship between father and son is movingly illustrated.

117. Kahana, R. J. (1981). The aging survivor of the Holocaust, discussion, reconciliation between the generations: A last chance. Journal of Geriatric Psychiatry, 14(2):225–239.

Reconciliation, or the resolution of conflicts between the generations, is seen as a criterion for successful adaptation in later life. This notion is based on Erikson's concept of ego integrity, according to which the adaptive goal of the final stage of life is expressed through the acceptance of one's one and only life cycle as something that had to be had and permitted no substitutions. It thus means a new, a different love of one's parents. The work of Sigmund Freud on his famous book, The Interpretation of Dreams, is cited for illustrating the importance of the concept of reconciliation with the past, and especially with a significant loss, such as a father's death. The author uses the case illustration given by Dr. Herzog for his analysis. Studies of survivors and their children are cited to emphasize the need for understanding the clinical implications of "survivor" and "transmission of trauma" in treating children of aged survivors.

118. **Krystal, H. (1981). The aging survivor of the Holocaust integration and self-healing in posttraumatic states. Journal of Geriatric Psychiatry, 14(2):165-188.**

Using available research on the disturbances survivors exhibit in their behavior, which renders them in general poor candidates for psychotherapy, the author describes his own experiences with about a thousand concentration camp survivors, who were requested to come in for a follow up by the German restitution authorities, or who sought consultation because of difficulties in their lives. A dozen of these patients were 78 years old and had been in psychoanalytic psychotherapy with the author. The relationship of certain posttraumatic constellations, and the survivors' revision in old age of their evaluation of their lives are the focus of this article. Old age requires an acceptance of the past as it unfolded. Those who cannot accomplish this task face the waging of an internal war against the ghosts of their past.

119. **Leon, G. R., Butcher, R. L., Kleinman, M., Goldberg, A. and Almagor, M. (1981). Survivors of the Holocaust and their children: Current status and adjustment. Journal of Personality and Social Psychology, 41(3):503-516.**

This comparative study evaluated the psychological adjustment of survivors of the Holocaust and their children with a control group of persons of similar European and religious background. Subjects included a total of 81 adults and 63 children. The Minnesota Multiphasic Personality Inventory (MMPI) was administered to all participants in the study. In addition, the Parent version of the Current Life Functioning Form in two versions, for adults and for children, was used as research instruments. Findings indicated that both groups' adjustment was within the normal range. Children in both groups expressed a general closeness toward their parents and a genuine concern about their welfare. These findings led the authors to conclude that notions of survivor guilt, emotional blunting, and maladaptive psychological influence of the survivors on their children have no real basis and should be rejected.

120. Merowitz, M. (1981). The aging survivor of the Holocaust,
Words before we go: The experience of Holocaust and its effect on
communication in the aging survivor. Journal of Geriatric Psychiatry, 14(2):241-244.

Effective communications with another person require many different abilities and elements which the experience of the Holocaust may completely disrupt. This experience may affect biology,
interfere with social labeling, assault the inner sense of continuity and community required for social learning, and may block
the reception of the message by the listener. The author focuses
on words that communicate, contain and tame experience. Words
help with the grieving, with bearing witness, and with renuncia-
tion of all those things that we can no longer perform or achieve.
Continuity of ceremony and roles, and knowledge that we did enough
and deserve a good rest are important elements of good mental
health in old age. Some survivors are able to find continuity
with goodness, but some others remain in the darkness.

121. Ornstein, O. (1981). The aging survivor of the Holocaust,
the effects of the Holocaust on life-cycle experiences: The
creation and recreation of families. Journal of Geriatric Psychiatry, 14(2):135-154.

The importance of parenting and its affect on the aging process
in the Holocaust survivor is discussed. Theoretical approach used
to explain differences in the psychology of survival is explicat-
ed. The author suggests that psychological recovery in survivors
depends on such factors as the pre-Holocaust personality organization, age at the time of incarceration, amount of time spent in
various camps, the physical conditions in the camps, and on the
frequency of moves from one camp to another. Kohut's theory of
the bipolar self, or motivation for the maintenance of continuity
and sameness, and the effect of parenting are further explanatory
factors on the processes of recovery. Two case illustrations are
provided in support of the author's conceptualizations. Parenting
is seen as an adult experience that can most fully restore the
survivor who has lost his or her original family.

122. Rosenbloom, M. (1985). The Holocaust survivor in late life.
Journal of Gerontological Social Work, 8(3-4):181-191.

Survivors of the Nazi era in occupied Europe during World War II
were for a decade a taboo subject, as society showed no interest
in them, and they responded by silence. In recent years, however,
there is a public awakening of consciousness which leads to the
aged Holocaust survivors as a unique group of people among the
aged population in the U.S.. Since professionals who work with

the aged can find significant lessons in the study of human behavior under extraordinary circumstances, a knowledge of the Holocaust is essential for them both for personal and professional
purposes. The remaining aged survivors of the Holocaust are
little known at present. They differ markedly in every respect,
as they came to this country from culturally heterogeneous communities in Europe. Even their personal experiences during the
Holocaust are individualistic, despite the camps, the ghettoes,
the hiding places or living among the partisan fighters of the
Nazis as each environment contained unique stresses and required
individual coping ability. Long term effects of the deprivations
and terrors suffered, while present in many, are not uniform either. The need for understanding their unique situation, and for
learning the most appropriate forms of care and intervention on
behalf of these survivors are discussed.

123. Steinitz, L. Y. (1984). Psychosocial effects of the Holocaust on aging survivors and their families. Journal of Jewish
Communal Service, 60(4):331-336.

Survivors of the Holocaust are largely aged by now. These
people consist of a special category for whom the conventional
judgments of clinicians of "good" or "bad" psychosocial adjustment
do not apply. In this exploratory study conducted with aging
survivors, with their children, and with 40 clinicians and researchers associated with the Group Project for Holocaust Survivors and their children, the unique reactions of the survivors to
the residual effects of the War's trauma were investigated. Issues of intergenerational communication, loss, long-term care for
the frail parent, and positive coping capacities are described,
and several treatment, program, and research implications are
raised.

Economic Distress, Crime, Sensory and Social Losses

124. Amir, M. and Bergman, S. (1976). Patterns of crime among
aged in Israel: A second phase report. Israel Annals of Psychiatry and Related Disciplines, 14(3):280-288.

This is a second phase of a 1973 study in which the criminality
patterns of Israeli persons 60 years old and older were examined,
using the 1960-1965 police records as data. The offenders' sex
and country of origin, their ecological distribution, and immigration patterns were taken into consideration in analyzing the
data. Findings indicated that the majority of the aged criminals
began their careers in crime at age 50 or older. Most often committed crimes were against property, persons and public order.
About one third of the older offenders were recidivists. Many
aged offenders tended to repeat the same type of crime, but only 8
percent of them were imprisoned. Methodological problems encountered in data analysis are elaborated.

125. Becker, D. G., Blumenfield, S. and Gordon, N. (1984). Voices from the Eighties and beyond: Reminiscences of nursing home residents. Journal of Gerontological Social Work, 8(1-2):83-100.

Thirty residents of the Jewish Home and Hospital for the Aged in New York City were interviewed. Trained volunteers taped the residents' life histories. Oral histories are used for life review therapy. These projects provide opportunities for the elderly to record their memoirs and contribute to historical data about different periods through the eyes and experiences of those who were personally involved in them. Common themes expressed by the participants included the joys and problems of the aged, while coping with and adapting to nursing home life were more individualistic. Guidelines for the institution of similar programs in other facilities are offered by the authors.

126. Berman, Y. (1974). Some problems of the aged in the rural milieu in Israel. International Journal of Aging and Human Development, 5(3):257-263.

Problems of the aged in Israeli rural settlements such as the Moshav, the Kibbutz and the Village are presented. Each of these settings has its unique history and a different approach to aging of its members. In all three, the elderly find that their previous status is being challenged due to social and cultural changes in the norms and values of the new generations.

Dependency problems are particularly painful. In the Moshav the aged who can no longer work in agriculture are dependent on their children and others for support. In the Kibbutz, status issues are dominant. Challenges to the rule of the elderly by the increasingly affluent young farmers pose particular problems for the old in the village. Integration of the aged in the Kibbutz stands in marked contrast to the social isolation of their peers in the Moshav. In all three societies the aged are on retreat and give way to the young.

127. Brodsky, I. (1977). Financing services to the aged: Approaches and dilemmas. Journal of Jewish Communal Service, 53(3): 261-267.

Many Jewish Community Centers are serving increasingly larger numbers of elderly as part of the demographic changes and population trends in the United States. Funding of services for this growing population is related to identifiable needs that arouse social concern. Increased allocation of funds for programs to the elderly are closely related to perceived priorities and to the results of fundraising activities. One of the persistent dilemmas in resource allocation is how to maintain those programs for which

initial funding came from grants when such grants are terminated.
Still another question is whether decision makers in the community
are adequately involved in project planning and implementation.
Two needs of the aged to which the Centers can contribute more
significantly in the future are continuing education and pre-
retirement counseling.

128. Edelson, J. S. (1976). The mentally impaired aged: Reorder-
ing priorities. Journal of Jewish Communal Service, 53(1):63-73.

Two specific projects and their results at the Jewish Home for
the Aged in Toronto, Canada are presented. Both projects concentrated on the grossly mentally impaired residents. Most of these
patients cannot manage by themselves their daily living. They are
unable to survive without continuous help and supervision. Delivering care to these people by nurses and social workers often
runs into great difficulties, as client behavior is largely unpre-
dictable. The special care demonstration project was concentrated
on one floor with 43 residents. During the course of this project
the focus shifted from activities to a supportive environment
tailored to the residents' abilities. The second project was a
training program for staff of Home working with mentally impaired
residents. Experience gained in the first project, and improvement in the quality of care following the training project are
discussed, and questions about assessment and diagnosis of mental
impairment are raised.

129. Goodman, A. C. and Hankin, J. R. (1984). Elderly Jews and
happiness with locale. Special Issue: Attachment to place. Population and Environment: Behavioral and Social Issues, 7(2):87-
102.

The satisfaction with and attachment to neighborhood were analyzed among 268 elderly urban Jews. Preference theory was used as
the conceptual framework in which attachment and satisfaction were
related to the consumption of goods and services. Findings indicated that bonds to place increased with age, while perception
of the neighborhood as an unsafe place decreased these bonds.
Stress associated with community change and the percentage of
Blacks in the neighborhood were significantly related to the bonds
with the locale and to decisions to relocate.

130. Huberman, S. (1986). Jews in economic distress. Journal of Jewish Communal Service, 62(3):197–208.

The new Jewish poverty is described using New York City and Chicago as illustrations. These two cities mounted comprehensive anti-poverty projects as a response to some alarming statistics: in New York City 13% of the Jewish population is poor, half of them are elderly yet, 62% of poor Jews do not report contact with Jewish agencies. In Chicago 15% are economically disadvantaged, and close to half of them (48%) are aged. The majority of poor Jewish elderly are older women. The rate of poverty among elderly Jews is increasing due to social welfare program cuts by the Federal government. At the same time philanthropy has not kept pace with the rising need for assistance. Ideas of what needs to be done to avert a crisis are offered.

131. Kahana, E. and Felton, B. J. (1977). Social context and personal need: A study of Polish and Jewish aged. Journal of Social Issues, 33(4): 56–74.

Interviews conducted with a sample of 402 older people living in a predominantly Polish or Jewish neighborhood with respect to their service needs reveal similarities despite their cultural and life-style differences. These needs are most acute in the areas of housing, health care, and finances. The problems facing researchers in studying ethnic aged are also reviewed.
Among these are instrumentation, access, and interpretation of the data. There are ethical issues as well, such as studying disadvantaged elderly without providing for their needs.

132. Morginstin, B. (1987). Long term care insurance in Israel. Ageing International, 14(2):10–13.

Long term care needs of the chronically ill, disabled elderly, who have become dependent on others for assistance with activities of daily living, has become a major concern in Israel for the past decade. One-third of all aged in Israel are 75 years old and older. They constitute the main population at risk requiring long term care services in home or at institutions. Recognition of their unique situation necessitated the introduction in the Israeli Parliament a law which created a Long-Term Care insurance branch within the framework of the Israeli social security system. The primary aims of this law, its major provisions, eligibility for services and benefits, and the method of its implementation are reviewed in this article.

133. Natow, A. B. and Heslin, J. A. (1982). Understanding cultural food practices of elderly observant Jews. Journal of Nutrition for the Elderly, 2(1):49-55.

Elderly observant Jews, usually Orthodox, but can belong to Conservative, and even Reform groups, live according to traditional beliefs and religious practices. Observant Jews have special food requirements. An explanation of the Jewish dietary law, or Kashrut, is given along with suggestions of how these practices may be adhered to, or what specific dietary modifications needed to provide quality health care and nutrition. Explanations of food products and consideration for institutional feeding are addressed.

134. Rosin, A. J. Abramowitz, L. and Diamond, J. (1985). Environmental management of senile dementia. Social Work in Health Care, 11(1):33-43.

A model of social activity geared to the needs of demented old people living in Israeli communities is presented. The program consist of transportation to and from the club, home assessment and follow-up visits, guided social interaction, physical activity, reality orientation, dance therapy and craftmanship. Coordinated with the local authority agencies, this program combines elements of support for the spouses as well. The daily activities involve collaboration among the educational and social services staffs and help patients to cope with a more meaningful social environment.

135. Sherwin, B. L. (1987). Euthanasia: A Jewish view. The Journal of Aging and Judaism, 2(1):35-57.

The question of which options obtain when two biblical notions collide with each other is discussed in this essay. Jewish tradition emphasizes the value of life, yet recognizes the inevitability of death. Euthanasia, or "easy death," has become a pertinent and a growing problem for patients, their families, and to an assorted array of practitioners in the helping professions. The author reviews and discusses Jewish religious, moral, and legal literature pertaining to euthanasia and cites Rabbinical sources for and against "easy death." Jewish sources have developed a variety of views to resolve the inevitable conflict between a commitment to the value of life, and a commitment to mitigate pain and suffering during the process of dying. While active euthanasia could be justified within the framework of Rabbinical teaching, the author also warns that each person involved must decide which of the two verses applies: "Choose Life" (Deut. 30: 19), or "There is a time to die" (Eccles. 3:2), and how the fulfillment of that verse may be implemented.

136. Shichor, D. and Bergman, S. (1979). Patterns of suicide among the elderly in Israel. The Gerontologist, 19(5):487-494.°

Patterns of suicide among the elderly in Israel were studied. Official statistics of completed and attempted suicide were analyzed as data. Findings revealed somewhat different patterns among these subjects than are known about the elderly in Western Industrial societies.

137. Shomaker, D. (1984). Economic pressures resulting from aging of Kibbutz society. The Gerontologist, 24(3):313-317.

Founders of the Kibbutzim, or the elderly utopian settlers and pioneers of this small but significant portion of Israeli society, came to build a communal settlement with Zionist and egalitarian ideals. Now they are aged and many became dependent on their own children and on younger members of the collective. While the zeal and ideological goals have not been drastically altered, the commitment to self-sufficiency is getting more and more difficult to maintain. The nonproductive members must find a role in the external economy to contribute to their own sense of self-worth and to the economy of the Kibbutz, as the rate of the young (under 19) and the old (65+) is on the rise. Since there is no retirement in the Kibbutz, yet there is a recognition of inevitable physical decline of the old, a gradual reduction in working hours is in effect. Old members opt for remaining in the labor force as long as they can to stave off boredom and to gain status. Health care needs of aged members are provided for internally with the resources of the Kibbutz as long as possible. When these are not sufficient for the frail and sick, they are augmented by external resources of the Workers' Union. Changes brought about by demographic trends have transformed the original ideals of the Kibbutz to a less self-sufficient and a more cooperative unit with the outside services and resources of the country.

138. Silfen, P. et al. (1977). The adaptation of the older prisoner in Israel. International Journal of Offender Therapy and Comparative Criminology, 21(1):57-65.

The question of whether or not aged prisoners need special units within the Israeli prison system was investigated. Subjects were 15 prisoners, aged 50 and over, each of whom was twice interviewed. The prisoners' future plans, self concept, relationships with others, and their dependence on inmates and wardens constituted one interview, while the second interview centered on general health, sexual activity, sleeping and eating habits, and etc.. The prisoners were classified according to their sources of equilibrium. Findings indicated the system's ability to meet halfway those prisoners who were unable to function independently in the prison. Therefore the idea of having special units within the prison for aged prisoners was rejected by the authors.

139. Silverberg, D. (1977). The "old" poor - and the "new" - what's happening to them? Present Tense, 4(3):59-64.

The plight of American urban Jewish poor is examined through the writings of noted scholars. Government and local community sources, including those of the Hasidic Jews, are cited.

140. Sweetbaum, S. (1966). A Jewish community center addresses the needs of the visually impaired older adult. Journal of Jewish Communal Service, 63(2):147-150.

Severe visual impairment, or blindness, is associated with diseases that afflict especially the aged. Over one million persons aged 65 years old and older suffer from the devastating effects of this malady. Coupled with additional hardships and losses that old age brings to seniors, the panic felt at becoming dependent on others is often a cause behind the blind person's withdrawal and isolation. Fears of falling, of being ridiculed, or pitied, prevent many blind older individuals from participation in Center programs. To combat this situation, a program, geared especially to the visually impaired, was developed by the staff of the Jewish Community Center of Greater Washington. Titled "Internal Light," the elements of this unique program enhance participants' knowledge of new skills, provide them with opportunities for socialization, and use outside help for increasing intergenerational relationships with the young and the sighted. The success of this program led to its replication at four sites elsewhere in Maryland.

Filial Responsibility and Communal Support

141. Bromberg, E. M. (1983). Mother-daughter relationships in later life: The effect of quality of relationship upon mutual aid. Journal of Gerontological Social Work, 6(1):75-92.

Using a sample of 75 mother-daughter pairs, the author set out to discover the affective quality of the relationships among them. All the mothers in this study were Jewish widows, age 65 years and over, who resided in New York City and whose daughters lived relatively close by to them. Patterns of helping and attitudes toward aging were also studied. Data collected by mailed questionnaires point to quite positive relationships among these mother- daughter pairs. Respondents rated their present relationships as stronger and as more satisfying than in the past, especially in terms of communication, mutuality and interdependence. The question whether these findings have any relationship to an increase in life expectancy of women is discussed.

142. Chernick, M. (1986).   Who pays?   The Talmudic approach to filial responsibility.   The Journal of Aging and Judaism, 1(2): 109–117.

To discover the spiritual message of the Talmud, one must search between the lines and analyze the cases and the arguments presented, for the Talmud's primary form of expression is cases, not high-sounding pronouncements. What is required from us with respect to our parents is explored in the text: Tractate Kiddushin 31b–32a. The analysis of the text, its Jewish implications, and the values and convictions of the rabbis who speak in the text are presented. Who pays for the care of an incapacitated old parent is a complex matter. It involves all the resources of both as well as their capabilities. It is also based on the intricacies of parent-child relations, which the Talmud has recognized long ago. There is much to learn from the way in which the Talmud deals with the question cited.

143. Gerrity, P. L.   By ourselves: An ethnographic study of self-care in an elderly Jewish population.   Doctoral dissertation, University of Pennsylvania, 1983.   Dissertation Abstracts International, 44(07):2244–A, Order No. DA 8326292.

Self care is defined as an initiative which individuals take on their own behalf with the specific expectation of health promotion and for the prevention and treatment of disease. Using an ethnographic approach, elderly Russian-Jewish former small business owners were interviewed. These people relocated from the inner city to an outlying urban neighborhood with the hope of spending there the remainder of their lives. Self-care was found to constitute a large portion of activity, and was based on deeply rooted cultural beliefs and shared peer experiences. The common background and values served as guide to their responses to pain and helped to provide content and purpose to their lives.

144. Goist, D. F.   "Will you still need me? Will you still feed me? When I'm 84."   Doctoral dissertation, Case Western Reserve University, 1980.   Dissertation Abstracts International, 41: 1119–A.

Based on three years of anthropological observations, two groups of elderly Jewish people in Leeds, England, and Cleveland, Ohio are examined as to their adjustment to an aged role. The group in Leeds is less anxious, less lonely and less uncertain about their role in their families than the group in Cleveland. Historical and sociological factors are explored to account for these differences in the behavior of the groups. Three factors are identified as helping the aged to adjust to role changes: the quality of earlier relationships within their family of orientation; the shared life-styles of aged parents and adult children, and the presence of life-long intimate friends. The importance of kinship roles for the adjustment of aged parents to old age are emphasized.

145. Harris, A. P. (1983). An exploration of the needs of Jewish patients and families in hospice programs in the greater Los Angeles area, 1982. Journal of Jewish Communal Service, 59(4): 326-330.

Hospice programs are growing in the United States at a rapid rate. In 1981 there were some 440 such programs and hundreds more were in development. Hospice program is a system of caring for the terminally ill. In 1982 the Jewish Hospice Commission of greater Los Angeles began a study to identify the needs of Jewish patients and their families for these programs as perceived by the caregivers. Five hospital based and nineteen mixed community/home care based hospice models were identified. These programs maintained an extensive and comprehensive linkage system with other services in the community to effect the transition of patient and family from in-patient to care in the home and back again. Some 3,000 patients used these facilities at the time the survey was taken. The needs of Jewish patients and their families were identified, but findings revealed that most hospices were frequently unable to provide them.

146. Hoffman, R. S. (1988). Aging, Judaism, and community. The Journal of Aging and Judaism, 2(3):175-179.

Judaic perspecetives on aging, and their relevance to Jewish communities are discussed. Medicine is singled out to highlight the importance of past teachings about health, disease, and life to modern approaches in health care. Illnesses and physical diseases are mentioned in the Torah not just for their own sake, but for their relationship to the moral and spiritual aims of Judaism. Holiness was equated with good health, while sin brought in its wake physical and mental breakdown. This relationship between body and mind was always recognized by Jewish physicians throughout the centuries and has become a maxim in modern medical practice as well. Changes in the spheres of science and demography within the past five decades have drastically curtailed the traditional roles of adult children as caretakers of aged parents and grandparents. There is a need to reaffirm the value of the community for the aged, to secure justice and provide for their welfare. Maintenance of the unique Jewish spiritual environment that provides meaningful and dignified old age, in line with the Jewish tradition, is advocated. Children should be taught "to look through the age mask and get past the physical aspects of

aging to the human being underneath," while the Jewish community
at large should prepare, plan, and courageously face the onslaught
of the millions of aged in their 80's, 90's, and even centenarians
that will appear on the horizon of the 21st century.

**147. Hollander, E. K. and Peyser, H. (1984).   Family volunteer
support group for Jewish aged in senior housing. Journal of Jewish Communal Service, 61(2):169-173.**

Relatives, friends, and tenants working together can make a
senior adult apartment building become a functioning community.
An illustration from such a housing in Washington, D.C. is given
to describe how to activate volunteer organizations and how to offer support and services to aged residents. The focus of the
volunteer group is on the encouragement and enhancement of independent living by the elderly, while their role is to serve as
facilitators in this process.

**148. Kart, C. S. and Engler, C. (1985).   Family relations of aged
colonial Jews: A testamentary analysis. Ageing and Society, 5
(3):289-304.**

Family relations of aged colonial Jews were reconstructed using
41 wills probated in New York between 1704 and 1799. Aged Jewish
colonial testators followed a familistic inheritance pattern regardless of their marital status, yet individual wills contained
at times vindictive and well articulated bequests. Modernization
theory is used to analyze these findings and their implications in
explaining adaptation of colonial Jews to a changing social cultural environment. The importance of comparative studies in the
history of the family relations of the aged is stressed by the
authors.

**149. Kravitz, L. S. (1987).   Who shall live and who shall die?
Who decides what is artifical prolongation of life?   A Jewish
view. The Journal of Aging and Judaism, 1(2):118-125.**

The issue of timing in dying at the "appointed time and not at
the appointed time" is raised. The first seems natural, as if the
individual has fulfilled his preordained measure, while the second
seems unnatural, as if the individual had been snatched untimely
away from life. In Jewish tradition, dying before one's time is
perceived sometimes as a benefit, and living longer is not always
a blessing. Illustrations from the Talmud are used to present
arguments for letting a person die when dying means the cessation
of unbearable pain and suffering, and when the prolongation of

life serves no purpose. The patient's condition, and the competence of the physician are discussed as additional factors in the decision to treat or not to treat a dying person. Positive and negative actions may be dependent on the level of technology, on the perceived level of the suffering of the patient, and on his will. Each case is unique, and each particular situation must be judged ethically by all concerned.

150. Kremer, Y. (1985). The association between health and retirement: Self-health assessment of Israeli retirees. Social Science and Medicine, 20(1):61-66.

Self-health evaluations and health behavior of 310 former industrial and service workers were compared with these workers retrospective self-assessments of health during their preretirement period. The hypothesis that retirement is responsible for worsening health conditions leading to overuse of medical services was contradicted by the findings. Normal biological aging processes, and not the life change retirement entails, are seen as factors in the decline in the perceived health state of these workers.

151. Kremer, Y. (1984-1985). Predictors of retirement satisfaction: A path model. International Journal of Aging and Human Development, 20(2):113-121.

The adjustment of 310 former industrial and service workers in Israel to retirement was studied using path analysis. The respondents indicated a general sense of coming to terms with the loss of work and enjoyed a more relaxed lifestyle. The retirees' evaluation of giving up work, activities with family and friends, rest and tranquility, and free time were the dominant variables in this path model, while situational, and behavioral variables, except for educational level and subjective state of health, had negligible effects on overall satisfaction with retirement.

152. Lucks, H. C. (1981). Widow/widower outreach program (WWOP): The social work role with members of mutual-help program and their families. Social Work Papers, 16: 82-89.

Widowed volunteers under the supervision of a social worker function as outreach personnel to the newly widowed elderly in the Jewish community of San Francisco. The volunteers offer emotional support and connect the newly widowed to the program. Expanding the friendships of these people with elderly in similar circumstances, and a supporting social network, may be valuable in confronting the variety of changes that widowhood brings to an individual and in preventing social isolation. The program offers consistency and structure to a population in a transitional crisis and helps relieving individual and family stresses resulting from widowhood.

153. Stern, M. H. (1986). When should a rabbi retire? The Journal of Aging and Judaism, 1(1):70-73.

Rabbis should adopt the maxim: always leave them laughing when you say good-bye. For many rabbis grow accostumed to the honors bestowed upon them by their congregations and forget to remember the time when one should gracefully retire. Retirement can be a rich and a happy period of a rabbi's career – if he knows how to use the free time well. There are plenty opportunities for continued service of the community as well, especially for those who wish to engage in volunteer activities. Retiring rabbis should get out of town, or find sufficient occupation away from the congregation, and plan for the 20 years of retirement that awaits them.

154. Weihl, H. (1981). On the relationship between the size of residential institutions and the well-being of residents. The Gerontologist, 21(3):247-250.

The effect of residential home size on the well-being of the residents was measured using social relations, attitude of the staff, feelings of loneliness, and overall satisfaction with residential home living as key variables. Subjects were one thousand residents in twenty one Israeli homes for the well aged. Findings revealed that residents of larger institutions (with over ninety beds) were more satisfied with the setting and the conditions there than did residents of smaller homes. Staff attitudes were influential in residents satisfaction especially in the smaller institutions.

155. Weinberg, J. (November, 1974). What do I say to my mother when I have nothing to say? Geriatrics, 29, pp. 155-159.

Adult children can learn much about their origins and identity by asking aging parents to reminisce. Honor and respect for one's parents, that are part and parcel of the Jewish tradition about the aged, imply honoring their mores and teachings. Communication with elderly parents means more than exchange of information. It means the acceptance of the parents' values, even when they differ from those of their children. Much communciation goes on nonverbally, through the senses. As a result, each person's view of himself and others may be confirmed, altered, or radically modified. What needs to be heard and understood is a person's yearning for affective interactions. By listening to tales of past we come to recognize and appreciate the uniqueness of another person's life.

156. Wolfe, C. (1985). Sharing information in the Jewish world aging network. Papers on Aging in the Jewish World. Draft for Comment AJW-19-85. The JDC-Brookdale Institute, Jerusalem, Israel.

The need for worldwide attention to the elderly as vulnerable populations in all societies is underscored by statistics on the alarmingly large increases expected in this population in this and the next centuries. There is a corresponding need for close cooperation and interaction by the world of Jewish communities everywhere. Common characteristics of the Jewish aging experience and their implications for professionals and services dealing with the needs of the Jewish elderly are cited and analyzed. Creating an international organization of agencies and professionals concerned with the Jewish aging is strongly recommended, and the various functions of this agency are listed. Opportunities for programming and for establishment of a small planning committee are suggested.

157. Woolf, L. (1985). The changing needs of the well elderly. Papers on Aging in the Jewish World. Draft for Comment, AJW-21-85. The JDC-Brookdale Institute, Jerusalem, Israel.

Changing needs of today's well aged will pose an unprecedented challenge and offer new vistas of services, the author states. The years between 50 and 75, or the third stage of life, will emerge soon as the prime time of life as professionals, artists, and others will continue working at the peak of their creative powers. Many older people will be exploring new careers, new interests, and new opportunities once their family raising roles have been completed. Improved health care and lack of debilitating illnesses will combine with vigorous exercises to preserve and to strengthen stamina and to keep this age group in good health. Policy makers and planners in the Jewish social services are cautioned to care for those who still live in poverty, and who will not be able to benefit from this new era. New service models catering to the well aged will have to be created, but the need to continue serving the frail aged will remain as pressing as at present.

158. Zlotowitz, B. M. (1986).   Should intermarriage be performed for the elderly?   Should one perform a marriage for an elderly couple who do not have a State License?   The Journal of Aging and Judaism, 1(1):68–69.

Problems related to intermarriage among the aged are raised from rabbinical perspectives.   Marriage is one of the most sacred institutions of Jewish life.   At whatever age it takes place, it fulfills one of the greatest Mitzvoth.   A rabbi cannot perform such marriage for two reasons, the author claims: one, that the bride or the groom who is a non-Jew does not believe in the words and the ancient formula of marriage, and is asked to participate in a ceremony that may violate his or her conscience, and two, that marriage without a state marriage license is tantamount of living together as husband and wife is done to preserve their individual social security benefits.   Under such conditions halachah prohibits the rabbi from performing a marriage, for the law of the land is supreme.   Potential or real economic suffering imposed on such a couple by existing social security laws cannot force a rabbi to commit an act of hillul hashem, a desecration of God's name.

5 Services Provision to Jewish Aged

Patterns and Methods in Services Delivery

159. Adelson, G., Kaminsky, P. and Cohen, C. J. (1979). Volunteers can help patients adjust. Health and Social Work, 4(1):184–199.

Trained volunteers provide valuable services to aging patients who are moving from an acute-care to a long-term care facility. These patients often feel abandoned by their family and the acute-care facility and are terrified at the change awaiting them. The Long Island Jewish-Hillside Medical Center has developed a program in which trained volunteers act as friendly visitors and as liaison between the patient and the facility or community agency, easing the pains of the transition for the elderly patient to the long-term care facility.

160. Cadigan, D. A. Health care utilization by the elderly: An application of the Andersen Model. Doctoral dissertation, The Johns Hopkins University, 1984. Dissertation Abstracts International, 45(11):3458-A, Order No. DA8501625.

Illness level, enabling and predisposing factors used in the Andersen model to predict outpatient and hospital utilization for a sample of 274 Jewish elderly were studied. All three groups of factors were significant predictors of health care utilization. Respondents with more education were more likely to have visited a physician. Being a member of a religious congregation, and being unmarried, significantly predicted the volume of physician visits, while age was inversely related to use. In this sample the Andersen model did not predict hospitalization well. An implication of these findings is that health service utilization should be considered only one of a number of possible responses to physical symptoms.

161. Carlowe, M. (1985). New and emerging service patterns within Jewish communal services for the frail and elderly. Papers on Aging in the Jewish World. Draft for Comment, AJW-5-85. The JDC-Brookdale Institute, Jerusalem, Israel.

Recent changes in the philosophy of services provision to the elderly in the United Kingdom, that emphasize a return to Victorian morality of independence and self-reliance, should force the Jewish social services community to reevaluate its dependence on State services and to begin planning for the needs of the frail elderly in particular. For these are the fastest growing population among the aged, and in the greatest need for Jewish communal services and supports. At present the State provides two-thirds of all expenditures for services to the Jewish aged. Should these funds be frozen or eliminated altogether, a real havoc would be created for Jewish social services to the aged. New patterns in serving the elderly include a greater emphasis on retaining independence and to live in dignity in the community by the provision of a continuum of services for both young, well, and frail elderly. Community centers and day care centers act as "youth clubs" for the aged. New methods of services delivery for keeping those who cannot benefit from these activities in the community are being developed. Residential homes have moved away from the nursing home model, and group living experiments are more frequently tried out along with other innovative new housing programs. Most importantly, the skills of the elderly are increasingly utilized in programming and in services delivery.

162. Carrilio, T. E., Cohen, R. G., and Goldman, A. R. (1980). The team method of delivering services to the elderly: An interim report. Journal of Jewish Communal Service, 57(1):56-62.

The Services for Older Persons unit at the Jewish Family Service of Philadelphia has a long and a distinguished service record. After working with individually offered service delivery methods by interested social workers, and with two member teams of bachelor level casework assistants, the agency has decided to expand its team concept and to venture into interdisciplinary teams. These consisted of both professional and paraprofessional staff. The teams' effectiveness was measured by the decrease in the need for institutional care. Differences between the conventional approach in service delivery and the team approach are elaborated. A study was undertaken to learn about the moral of the staff and client satisfaction with the new approach. Preliminary findings presented indicate the possible benefit of social work teams in working with clients who need concrete supports and counseling.

163. Fleishman, R. and Shmueli, A. (1984). Patterns of informal
social support of the elderly: An international comparison. The
Gerontologist, 24(3):303-312.

Affective and instrumental mutual supports among the aged and
their primary helpers were studied. Subjects residing in one of
the neighborhoods of Jerusalem, Israel were compared to those
found in similar Israeli and foreign studies. Findings revealed
strong patterns of mutual supports and minimal participation by
nonkin. While these findings are rather characteristic of com-
parable foreign studies, the elderly in Britain, Denmark, Holland,
Poland and the United States reported substantial assistance from
nonkin as well. Family-based informal support systems, the authors claim, can be used as complements to formal services. They
may also serve as alternatives to premature institutionalization
of the frail elderly.

164. Fogel, C. (1980). Reaching out to the aging through vocational services. Journal of Jewish Communal Service, 56(4):341-
343.

Employment and vocational rehabilitation needs of the Jewish
aged can be met through special services, such as the Jewish Vocational Service Work Center on Aging of Metropolitan New Jersey.
This service is considered successful as it provides remunerative
work to residents of a Home for the aged. Work and professional
supervision are provided by the service, while space and produc-
tion personnel are provided by the Home. Started with 16 client
residents, the program served at the time this article was written
more than 100 a week. Clients served in the program range in age
from 55-92. They benefit from many services. The support system
offered by the Work Center and its staff enable clients to stay in
the community even when they suffer traumas of losses and serious
illnesses. Vocational services are not limited to matters of employment and training but cater to a wide range of human needs.

165. Fuld, J. (1985). Jewish communal planning of services for
the elderly in small Jewish communities. Papers on Aging in the
Jewish World. Draft for Comment, AJW-12-85. The JDC-Brookdale
Institute, Jerusalem, Israel.

Significant aspects of the Jewish communal planning process in
serving small American and Canadian Jewish communities are explored. These include the diverse characteristics of small Jewish
cities, steps in the planning process, program development, and
the role of the outside consultant. Small communities are defined
as those having less than 5,000 Jewish individuals. Difficulties

of these communities in planning and programming are attributed to
their limited fiscal, organizational and personnel resources.
Smaller Jewish communities have strengths that are often overlook-
ed. These are identified, and means to exploit these ever further
are offered.

166. Goldstein, R. (1982). Adult day care: Expanding options for
service. Journal of Gerontological Social Work, 5(1/2):157-168.

Day care programs for the aging are seen as providing the elderly option for a more meaningful life in the community and as a
viable alternative to institutionalization. They are particularly
helpful to the isolated, marginally functioning aged who wish to
remain independent, people for whom there are only scant services
at present. Many frail elderly need care for various degrees of
dementia. Existing communal services cater mainly to the well
elderly and do not attract disabled clients. As a consequence,
many elderly people with special needs fail to benefit from these
services. Small day care programs that offer medical and psychosocial monitoring and intervention, social and rehabilitation
services are best able to meet the needs of both the family and
the elderly in preventing premature institutionalization.

167. Harel, Z. and Harel, B. B. (1978). Coordinated services for
older adults in the Jewish community, Journal of Jewish Communal
Service, 54(3):214-219.

Changes in the older adult Jewish population in terms of size,
economic, social and health characteristics, and vulnerability to
environmental stress are noted. These changes lead to a greater
reliance on formally organized services on the part of the older
person. Planning, development, and delivery of services for older
members of the Jewish community need to be more comprehensive.
Coordination among Jewish agencies serving the aged, broad community representation on planning boards, and involvement of the
older service consumers are seen as remedies in dealing with the
needs of the aged.

168. King, S. (1983). The family agency as a community base for
long term care. Journal of Jewish Communal Service, 59(4):331-
339.

Long term care refers to services provided to the frail elderly
by social and health care agencies either within their own homes,
in community settings, or in residential care homes, as well as in
institutions. Their common goal is the avoidance of premature institutionalization. Experiences of the Jewish Family Service site

in the State of California research and demonstration project in long term care titled the Multipurpose Senior Services Project (MSSP) are described. The long range goal of the MSSP is the provision of such services to all frail elderly. The case management team approach, which offers each client on-going relationship of a social worker and a nurse, is the basis of the project design. Conclusions derived from the operation of the MSSP are used by the Jewish Family Service to improve services delivery to the frail aged, and to plan more adequately future programs on their behalf.

169. Kollar, N. R. (1988). Interfaith coalitions and the crisis of the elderly: A practical solution. The Journal of Aging and Judaism, 2(4):221-236.

Religious institutions' relationships with the elderly are described in great detail. The need for increased partnership between the fast increasing elderly population and between the religious institutions is stressed as mutually rewarding as the aged need these institutions, and they in turn need them. It is in their common interest to work toward a favorable outcome. Interfaith coalitions should work together to shape national and local policies, to provide care for and with the elderly, to advocate institutional openness to religion, to offer religious education, and to serve as advocates for the aged. A model of potential interfaith advocacy is presented with a description of its goals, Board structure, meetings, research and finances.

170. Linzer, N. and Lowenstein, L. (1987). Autonomy and paternalism in work with the frail Jewish elderly. The Journal of Aging and Judaism, 2(1):19-23.

Autonomy in politics refers to independent self-rule without external interference, while paternalism is the principle or system of governing or controlling a country, group of employees, etc., in a manner suggesting a father's relationship with his children. These two concepts have been prominent in the medical ethics literature in recent years, as advances in medical technology led to increased longevity of people in general. Use of life extending devices created ethical conflicts for both doctors and social workers. The conflicts center on Jewish and professional perspectives concerning attitudes to the frail aged. A case is provided to illustrate the social worker's dilemma. According to the author the autonomy-paternalism conflict depicted in the medical ethics literature centers on life and death issues. It also exists in situations of daily living and involves a large array of people, whose involvement is described in Project Ezra.

171. Mitelpunkt, R., Baum, S. and Dasberg, H. (1981). Intervention in psychosocial compensation of the elderly in poor neighborhoods in Jerusalem. International Journal of Social Psychiatry,
27(4):271-275.

Efforts of a mental health center located in the northern section of Jerusalem vis-a-vis the elderly are described. Older
patients with acute psychological disorders are treated with
crisis intervention techniques. This community based program
offers a situational approach to the condition of the elderly.
Through collaboration with, and referral to various social and
health care agencies, the needs of the elderly patients are met.
In most cases the interventions are sufficient to reduce sympto-
matology and to restore healthier levels of functioning by the
aged. Case materials are provided to highlight the treatment
given to patients at this center.

172. Moss, M. S. and Pfohl, D. C. (1988). New friendships: Staff
as visitors of nursing home residents. The Gerontologist, 28(2):
263-265.

Staff at the Philadelphia Geriatric Center initiated a unique
program of visiting elderly residents of nursing homes in whose
care they were not personally or professionally involved.   Both
the visitor and the visited reported satisfaction with the weekly
meetings. The former saw in the visit an opportunity to create a
special friendship with an aged person, and a way to really learn
about the aging process, while for the latter the visits provided
an outlet for pent-up feelings, enhanced social status within the
nursing home, an expanded social network, and a heightened self-
esteem. The value of the program for the agency, and guidelines
for initiating similar programs elsewhere are described.

173. Prager, E. H. (1986). Community caring for the family caregiver: The development of a video outreach program in Israel.
Journal of Jewish Communal Service, 63(1):49-58.

Adult children and spouses are the primary caregivers to
frail elderly people in many countries. In Israel the still pre-
vailing social norms of filial responsibility, and the relative
absence of physical dispersion among elders and their kin make
caregiving by the younger generation a regular pattern of behavior. Many of these caregivers are middle aged or even "young
old" themselves with their own needs for care, and with responsibilities toward their own children. At times, their declining
physical, economic, and emotional capacities prevent them from
fulfilling their traditional obligation of caring for the aged
parent. Demographic changes have created a large and a rapidly

aging population in Israel, but services for their needs lag behind. The middle generation needs educational and supportive
guidance to help it cope effectively with its tasks. A unique
video program titled the "Family Care Guidance" project was
initiated in Israel in 1982 to alleviate feelings of alienation,
resentment, and helplessness among younger family caregivers. The
main objectives of this program are described in this article.

**174. Rathbone–McCuan, E. (1976). An experimental geriatric group
home. Journal of Jewish Communal Service, 53(3):301–308.**

The efforts of the Levindale Hebrew Geriatric Center and Hospital in creating a continuum of services to meet the needs of individuals with varying levels of functional capacity are described.
Among the innovative services that Levindale has pioneered is the
Hurwitz House Group Home. This facility in the community was designed to allow elders to live in the community under a modified
nursing home service pattern and with supervision, rather than to
be institutionalized due to their multiple frailties. A study
conducted to assess the effectiveness of this setting and approach
to caring is presented. The group home is compared with a similar
level of inpatient care. Results indicate that Hurwitz House
should be reserved for the more independent and motivated individual, or to those moderately motivated whose families are available
to provide the necessary linkages with the services in the community.

**175. Rothstein, D. G. (1983). Developing a voluntary, neighbor-
hood intergenerational program. Journal of Jewish Communal Service, 60(1):48–52.**

Two agencies in New York's south Bronx developed a joint
intergenerational program, in which they brought together young
and old people. The purpose of the program was to break down
racial and religious barriers and to fulfill the emotional needs
of the aged. Despite the difficulties encountered in finding
suitable funding for the program, the enthusiasm of the volunteers
can compensate for the lack of material resources. Interdependence between the young and the aged can strengthen relationships
and bring new dimensions to community development efforts.

**176. Rotter, F. (1988). An ecological approach to work with
Jewish older adults. The Journal of Aging and Judaism,
2(3):162–174.**

The ecological approach is concerned with transactions of
individuals with their environments. The objective is to obtain a
better "fit" by enhancing adaptive capacities and environmental
resources. The Life Model, based on operationalization of the

ecological perspective, can help workers understand how clients
deal with life stresses and their consequences. Judaism contains
means to recreate a sense of purpose, place and belonging, which
are at times threatened by the changes, family mobility, and weakening of the natural and communal support systems for many older
adults in modern life. Both the Life Model and the traditional
values of Judaism can be used by workers in assessing and treating
older individuals. Two tools that can help the assessment are the
genogram and the ecomap. These are pictorial representations done
together by client and worker. Genogram facilitates the life
review process, while the ecomap is used to identify the client's
supportive networks and how he or she functions in the current
life space. Case examples are offered for illustration of the
above, along with principles of practice, modalities of treatment
and conclusion.

177. Schneider, M. (1980). Cooperative planning for discharge
from geriatric institutional care. Journal of Jewish Communal
Service, 56(4):358-360.

A coordinated effort between a Jewish Family and Children Service and between a Hebrew Home and Hospital for the Aged is described. While the intake function for the community old age home
by the family agency is an accepted practice, especially in homes
without a social service department, it is unusual to perform the
discharge function. The two agencies agreed that in light of the
nursing home's policy of admitting short-term rehabilitation patients, a family service worker will be integrated into the institution to offer the family and the client continuity of service.
This worker meets the client and his or her family on the day of
admission, and begins working with them quickly. The functions of
this worker in the nursing home setting are identified, and ave-
nues for cooperation between this professional and the staff of
the home are discussed. This cooperation between the two agencies
is seen in the community as an effort to offer a continuum of services to clients, rather than to find an "only" solution to their
problems.

178. Seltzer, M. M., Simmons, K. Ivry, J. and Litchfield, L.
(1984). Agency-family partnership: Case management of services
for the elderly. Journal of Gerontological Social Work, 7(4):57-
73.

The Jewish Family and Children's Services of Boston, Massachusetts, instituted a research and demonstration project in which
partnerships were formed between agency social workers and family
members of elderly clients. The former were responsible for counseling and for providing support to the elderly client, while the
latter was taught to assume responsibility for case management.

During the first year of this 3 year project, several practice issues emerged. These are described in detail. Of special interest
are two questions: (1) whether the findings can be generalized to
other non-sectarian agencies? and (2) whether this model of intervention will survive beyond the life of the project?

**179. Shain, D. D. (1977). Group counseling with Jewish elderly.
Journal of Jewish Communal Service, 53(4):383-386.**

Counseling Jewish elderly to cope with personal and social problems is a core service at the Jewish Family Service in Philadelphia. Group members come usually once a week to the agency and
engage in discussions that center on the realities of their living
circumstances. Many members are widows. Some have marital problems, and others are ill. Loss of role identity is common among
these people. Members are encouraged to support and to maintain
contacts with each other outside the scheduled group activities.
Criteria for selection of group counselors; rationale for member-
ship selection, and the various stages of group work are discussed. Members are helped to restructure their identities, to set
goals, to re-connect with Jewish reverence for age, and to play
constructive roles in the lives of other group members.

**180. Singer, A. (1979). "Griefwork" and social group work with
senior adults in a Jewish community center. Journal of Jewish
Communal Service, 56(3):254-260.**

A social group for elderly parents who lost a middle-aged child
was formed at the Jewish community centers of South Florida. This
group helped grieving parents to resolve their "griefwork," which
the author considers as essential for going on living. Within
Jewish tradition and rituals, the emphasis is on avoidance of
excessive grief, self pity, and guilt due to the loss, and on
gradual returning to normal life. Criteria affecting griefwork,
and the rate of healing, are presented. These center around both
past and present strengths and supports that the bereaved person
can rely on when such a major emotional loss occurs. Social workers, counselors, and all others who work with the bereaved among
the aged, should be aware of these criteria.

**181. Solomon, J. R. (1980). Innovative outreach approaches in
services to the elderly. Journal of Jewish Communal Service, 56
(4):344-347.**

Innovative approaches taken in the community service programs of
the Miami Jewish Home and Hospital for the Aged are discussed.
These efforts are aimed at forestalling institutionalization and
to improve the quality of life for the elderly in the community.

Since the elderly suffer from a variety of problems which have a combined social and health genesis, there is a need to integrate the social and the health aspects in the delivery system. The "SWAT" team, standing for Service Workers for Aged in Trouble, and modeled after the police SWAT team, is a 3 year demonstration project which was put into effect at the Jewish Home. It uses modern technology in services delivery, and creates a sense of hope for continued independence of the elderly in the community. SWAT's primary methods of procedure include case management, and filling the gaps in social and health care services. The three innovative approaches used by the team include Lucy Booth, modeled after the "Peanuts" cartoon in which Lucy provides psychiatric help for five cents, training non-professional personnel to recognize problems in their older patrons, and reaching into nursing homes and congregate facilities to provide services.

182. Vinokur-Kaplan, D., Cibulski, O., Spero, S. and Bergman, S. (1981). "Oldster to oldster": An example of mutual aid through friendly visiting among Israeli elderly. Journal of Gerontological Social Work, 4(1):75-91.

The Israeli Social Security Administration has a well established network of friendly visitors to the elderly in every major city of the country. These visitors serve as volunteers, receive "in-service-training" on the job through workshops and lectures, and bring to the attention of social workers cases and problems encountered during their visits with the socially isolated, frail and home-bound elderly. Interviews with 94 of these friendly visitors revealed that they are seen as positive factors in improving the morale of the elderly in their care. Friendly visitors gain self esteem and a sense of usefulness by performing their tasks.

183. Weiner, M. (1986). Group treatment with aged. Journal of Jewish Communal Service, 62(4):307-317.

Group treatment with the aged is seen not as substitute for missing relationships and defective social linkages in the lives of the aged. Rather, group treatment is a partial compensation for some deficit in the life of an aged client. Aging is perceived by the author as a developmental phase in which the aged person must adjust to changes that are inevitable in a positive way. Diminution of independence and loss of control over one's environment and social status are connected losses. If work is not available, adequate family relations can support a continuous sense of self. Validation of the self may come from one's reference group as well. For many aged persons it is easier to relate to one's cohort than with others, for shared memories, language and customs are part of being in a cohort. The type of group

treatment used in the Jewish family services of Detroit is based
on a psychodynamic model in which relationships and processes provide the "growth medium". Clients are helped to recognize, identify and express feelings. The goal is to change patterns of behavior that interfere with the individual's sense of self-worth
and productive use of self in relationships.

184. Zweibel, N. R. (1984). Analysis of family decision-making in
selection of alternatives to institutionalization: A tool for
service planners and providers.   Conference Paper (150) 20p.:
Paper presented at the Annual Scientific Meeting of the Gerontological Society (37th San Antonio, TX., November 16-20, 1984).
Journal Announcement: RIESEP85

Interviews with 36 family caregivers revealed six alternatives
most frequently considered by families to prevent permanent institutionalization of their frail elderly members: long-term care,
companions, supportive congregate housing, counseling, in-home
services, and independent housing.   One in four families had
sought alternatives which were unavailable, while a little over
one-third of the respondents indicated that cost was a barrier to
services.   The aged relative refused in a few instances at least
one of the options considered, and close to two-thirds of the
families in this study reported a conflict within the family with
respect to the alternatives considered.   These and other findings
led the Council for Jewish Elderly to plan for the changing needs
of the Jewish elderly in its care.

Programs: New, Old, and Emerging

185. Arnowitz, D. I. (1980). What a summer vacation program means
to nursing home residents. Journal of Jewish Communal Service, 56
(4):353-357.

Residents in a home for the aged suffer from many ailments.
They often face the prospect of remaining at the facility for an
indefinite period of time.   A common disability afflicting many
residents is mental illness, which is partly the result of prolonged social isolation.   There is a possibility to counteract
this illness by providing strong psychological and social supports, and by altering the negative self image of the residents
with a positive one.   A program which is geared toward this goal
uses summer vacation for these residents in a camp.   Participants
gain a whole new appreciation of life and care by the staff.   Some
show a new interest in other residents.   Video taping of the program during the second summer gave staff, the residents, and their
families opportunities to reminisce about the time spent together.
It also served the purpose of evaluating the program for further
enhancements.   New types of programming, and experiencing new
roles by both professional and volunteer staff, are additional
benefits of this program.

186. Bendel, J. P. and King, Y. (Spring, 1985). Sheltered housing for the elderly in a multigenerational setting. Ageing International, 12(1):13-14.

A "success story" in sheltered housing, this project lcoated in a multigenerational setting on the outskirts of Jerusalem houses 59 older persons in ground-floor apartments. These residents have some unique supportive facilities. They all moved to this neighborhood to improve their housing standards. In the 18 months of this project, they developed important intergenerational relationships with the younger residents. When surveyed, both young and old reported on the benefits of mutual assistance and had favorable comments about this innovative housing project. Duplication of this program elsewhere in the country is advocated by the staff assigned to work with the residents.

187. Cohen, M. G. (November, 1975). Rehabilitation and day care: Another alternative. Maryland State Medical Journal, 71-73.

This article describes a rehabilitation program with 109 persons who were served over a four year period in the Levindale Hebrew Adult Treatment Center in Baltimore, Maryland. The program was based on a joint effort of cooperation between health and social service agencies in the community. Costly institutionalization of physically impaired older adults was either delayed or significantly limited for the majority of the participants in this program.

188. Duhl, J. (1983). An advocacy coalition of older persons. Journal of Jewish Communal Service, 60(1):44-47.

Older persons should have an opportunity to participate in public policy development and in legislation to preserve and to enhance their quality of life. Social agencies can facilitate the attainment of this goal by launching a vigorous effort of senior citizen advocacy. JASA, or the Jewish Association for Services for the Aged, provides social services to more than 50,000 elderly people annually. Its social coalition initiated in 1977 attempts to stimulate community interest in the problems of the elderly and helps them to become active advocates on their own behalf in health, income and social services delivery.

189. Eckerling, S., Bergman, R., Golander, H., Sharon, R. and
Tomer, A. (1986). Implications for architectural and structural
characteristics of institutions for the aged in Israel. International Journal of Nursing Studies, 23(4):349-362.

Physical characteristics of hospitals and long-term care facilities can have beneficial or detrimental effects on the care of the
elderly. They can promote social interaction and general satisfaction of the patients/residents, or reduce these significantly.
The importance of communal space, such as public gardens, which
the mobile aged tend to frequent, has been found repeatedly by researchers. In 1980 Israel had about 12,500 beds for long-term
geriatric care, yet this number was barely able to accomodate half
of the aged in need of long-term institutional care. The study
reported here included 35 facilities for the care of the aged in
central Israel. Its purpose was to discover needed changes in
architectural design to permit future institutions to learn from
the shortcomings of the presently available in the country. An
assessment tool was developed for rating of the participating institutions in the study in terms of the services available (or
lacking) on the premise. The findings revealed many implications
for immediate and future improvement of patient care, which could
be achieved through changes in architectural and structural de-
signs.

190. Eichler, M. (1977). Report from Israel. Journal of Geriatric Psychiatry, 10(2):243-248.

This report summarizes the status of treatment programs for
geriatric patients in Israel in the mid-seventies. Data are based
on epidemiological and clinical studies. A marked increase in the
percentage of elderly patients who receive treatment is noted over
a ten year period. Female patients far outnumber males, as in
other industrialized countries. The superiority of treatment provided in specialized geriatric units is stressed over treatment in
general medical units. Psychiatric problems among geriatric
patients are attributed mainly to loss of a spouse and to social
isolation.

191. Frankel, P. and Golant, M. (1981-82). A family life education program for Soviet Jewish seniors. Journal of Jewish Communal Service, 58(3):223-230.

Seventeen percent of the new immigrants from the Soviet Union
who have been resettled in Chicago are in the age range of 65-80
years. These people have a particularly difficult time adjusting
to life in America, as they have to cope with acquisition of a new
language, a new life style and a new culture simultaneously. The
Jewish Family and Community Service in Chicago has developed a

family life education program to ease the integration of Soviet seniors into the general and the Jewish community.   Details of this time limited, yet successful program are provided.

192. Fried, H. and Waxman, H. M. (1988).   Stockholm's cafe: A unique day program for Jewish survivors of concentration camps. The Gerontologist, 28(2):253-255.

Of the approximately 10,000 central and southern European Jews, who were brought to Sweden for convalescence after they survived the concentration camps of Nazi Germany, some 4,000 individuals remained there to start a new life.   Now, 45 years later, many of them suffer from nightmares, depression, fears of persecution, and from other symptoms.   The Jewish community in Stockholm has decided to create a unique program for these aged.   A cafe from the pre-war years was born.   Altogether about 80 people are served by this unique service.   Patrons enjoy the warmth and understanding of the staff, and have an opportunity to socialize with others. The combined approach of an informal group setting and non-confrontational treatment techniques resulted in relief of some symptoms.

193. Friedman, H. H. (1984).   Changes in programming for the Jewish aged in residential health care facilities.   Journal of Jewish Communal Services, 60(4):324-330.

A study of the characteristics of 127 Jewish residential health care facilities reveals a trend toward a decreasing number of facilities with solely Jewish patients, and an increasing number of facilities having a pluralistic patient population.   At the same time the present residents come from higher socioeconomic levels than ever before; are better educated, and have a serious interest for involvement in societal issues of the day.   Previous programs of activities were oriented toward "arts and crafts," religious services, and weekly movies.   These, however, do not satisfy the new type of residents.   Changes in programming must be undertaken to meet the cultural, educational and recreational needs of these residents, while continuing to uphold Jewish traditions and ideals.

194. Kaplan, F. (1981).   The senior center and the dying.   Journal of Jewish Communal Service, 58(1):123-132.

A pioneer program sponsored jointly by three Jewish communal services to combine group, supportive, and adjunctive services and individual treatment to seniors sensing their approaching death was developed and operated at the Jewish Family Service in Chicago.   Staffs from these agencies function as a team and offer a

wide variety of services to members of this group. The roles of
the social worker are described. They include the facilitation of
adjustment to the program, dealing with problems of dependency,
and offering protection and understanding to members. Creative
programming, and attention to individual needs, enhance the quality of life of both members and staff.

**195. Kartman, L. L. (1977). The use of music as a program tool
with regressed geriatric patients. Journal of Gerontological
Nursing, 3(4):38-42.**

At the Levindale Hebrew Geriatric Center and hospital in Baltimore, Maryland, two groups of impaired residents were given music
therapy: the first group was physically regressed and the second
was physically and emotionally regressed. The differential effects of music therapy with these patients are described in this
article.

**196. King, S. (1977). Counseling the young elderly: A responsive
approach, Journal of Jewish Communal Service, 54(1):26-31.**

The "young elderly" are persons in their 60's and early 70's,
who have very different characteristics and needs from individuals
in their late 70's, 80's or 90's. At times, and with increasing
frequency, the young elderly may even represent a different generation within the same family. This paper describes the work of
the Jewish Family Service in Los Angeles with a special "store-
front" operation. Three programs are outlined as methods of
counseling particularly appropriate for use with many younger
elderly clients. These are: 1) the Jewish family life development group; 2) the "coping group", and 3) the insight oriented
therapy group.

**197. Koff, T. H. (1974). How to start a day care program — and
make it grow. Modern Nursing Home, 32(1):33-34.**

The beginnings and growth of a day care program are described.
Opened with one patient in the Handmaker Home for the Jewish Aged
in Tucson, Arizona, the program has grown to three hundred patients in four centers. This article also offers information on
staffing a day care program and encourages interested nursing
homes to establish such a program.

198. Kostick, A. (February, 1974). Levindale day care program. The Gerontologist, 14:31-32.

A day care program conceived by the author to serve physically and mentally impaired community residents was instituted at the Levindale Hebrew Home and Geriatric Center in Baltimore, Maryland. The purpose of the program was to serve older persons who had less functioning capacity than senior center participants. Transportational services for program participants were provided. Each person could maintain his or her own physician while using the Center's facilities.

199. McCeney, E. (1985). Meals on Wheels for kosher clients in central Maryland. Journal of Nutrition for the Elderly, 5(1):61-64.

Observing the Jewish Dietary law means using foods that are fit for consumption in accordance with the Torah and its commentaries. Many elderly Jews have been raised on this age-long tradition and adhere to its implementation even under the changed conditions of living at times in a non-Jewish environment. Keeping this tradition in mind, the kosher menu for Meals on Wheels clients in central Maryland provides a variety of foods for lunch and for dinner which are in accordance with the necessary time limits between the consumption of meat and dairy foods. Fish, for example, can be served as either a hot or a cold meal since it is pareve. Thus, it is a favorite dish for Jewish elderly. The service takes into consideration the special diets and menus of the clients for holidays and assist families in adapting the weekend meals to a low sodium and/or diabetic diet.

New regulations in the State of New York require each facility to make a kosher diet available to patients/residents who desire to observe Jewish dietary law. This regulation necessitates the formulation of a written diet plan to be included in the facility's diet manual and a procedure for its implementation. Described is a nursing home which did not have a kosher kitchen and which had to institute new policies and procedures for the implementation of this requirement. Important points that must be considered to application of kosher food service are listed, and a diet manual is offered which includes the menu guidelines and the principles pertaining to kosher food. These guidelines can serve as a model for other non-kosher facilities for the implementation of the new law.

200. Novick, L. J. (1976).   A day-hospital program for brain-damaged confused geriatric patients.   Journal of Jewish Communal Service, 53(1):74-80.

Initiated in 1974 as a pilot project within an already existing day-hospital for mentally alert geriatric patients, this day-hospital for the brain-damaged at Maimonides Hospital and Home for the Aged in Montreal, Canada, sought to maintain such patients at their own homes and avoid placing them in institutions by rendering services geared to their specific needs. At first the professional staff was apprehensive about this plan and resisted their admission, but this resistance was overcome. Criteria that govern admission of an applicant to this day-hospital program for confused patients are cited, and the operations of the program are specified. Activities to involve the patients center on both menial and intellectual functioning. Small groups of patients are led by specially trained personnel.

Behavioral modification techniques and structuring the activities are utilized to encourage patients to utilize their remaining abilities. The day hospital tries to involve the relatives of these patients to continue maintaining them at home by relieving the relative of the burden of caring for the patients during the day. A trained social worker provides consultation services as needed by the families.

201. Peyser, H. and Jacobson, E. (1987).   "Special" volunteers in a home for the aged.   Journal of Jewish Communal Service, 64(2): 171-178.

At the Hebrew Home of Greater Washington an innovative, albeit risky, program was developed. In the over 600 volunteers a year, who fulfill many functions in the Home in providing direct and indirect services to the residents, a new, "special" volunteer emerged. This volunteer is a handicapped person, who can be either mentally retarded, learning disabled, or mentally ill. During the past year 12 such volunteers have worked in the Home. Six case studies, representative of the failures and successes of this innovation in the use of volunteers are presented. While the utilization of these volunteers is time consuming, the staff agrees that it is worth the effort. For through the volunteer activities at the Home, many handicapped individuals are given their first chance for a meaningful and productive life.

202. Reingold, E. (1982).   Helping elderly victims of crime.   Journal of Jewish Communal Service, 58(3):245-248.

Large number of Jewish aged are survivors of the Holocaust, or escapees from vicious anti-Semitism in their countries of origin. They have in common a fear of violence, a low sense of self-confidence, and memories of traumata suffered in the past. Many elder ly Jews living in large urban communities are highly vulnerable to crime due to their frailty and helplessness. The community based crime victims assistance program, established by the Jewish Association for Services to the aged in New York City, acts to help elderly Jews deal with the havoc wreaked on their lives by crime and violence. The program mobilizes greater community awareness about the needs of the elderly victim of crime. Social workers assigned to such programs need to be skillful in helping the victims, and in changing the community into a safe environment for the elderly.

203. Schneider, M. (1976). Small group home projects for the elderly. Journal of Jewish Communal Service, 53(1):88-92.

Small group home is a service that was born out of the inability of foster care homes and programs for the elderly to meet the demands for protective shelter. Many elderly simply cannot meet the requirements of foster care, especially if they are withdrawn, or cannot relate to family roles. Small group homes are especially suited to elderly without serious mental impairments who need protective settings. The program has community acceptance. There are no problems in renting an apartment for this purpose. It is non-threatening to adult children, as they feel less guilty about placing their parents in this setting. The elderly tenants also benefit from the program. It increases their sense of independence, and provides them with opportunities to assist in the running of the home.

204. Siegel, M. K. (1980). Arts and crafts as authentic experience for older people. Journal of Jewish Communal Service, 56 (4):348- 352.

Arts and crafts activities at the Center provide opportunities for engaging in creative experiences by older members. It is a means for involving people in social, artistic and intellectual activities; to enhance their self-esteem; to provide them with pride and satisfaction by producing things of beauty, and to increase their creative capacities. These activities are sources of pleasure. The meaning of creativity is discussed using illustrations from the works of philosophers, psychologists, and others. Discovering creativity through leadership benefits the skilled worker who teaches the elderly client. It taps the creativity of both. It strengthens the self-confidence of the elderly student, and it encourages him to work towards self-actualization.

205. Warach, B. (1986). Supportive services in housing for the
elderly: Emerging needs and problems. Journal of Jewish Communal
Service, 62(4):299-306.

Development of housing at affordable rent and with adequate and
appropriate supportive services are major objectives of Jewish
services for the aged. The great increase in the proportion of
the old (75 years and over) and especially of the very old (85
years and over) pose a special problem from managers of housing
complexes for the elderly. Supportive services within these complexes were geared mainly to the well elderly. They were designed
as community facilities and not as nursing or group home services.
Major problems of aging housing facility residents include chronic
illness, physical impairment and mental disability. Social workers have been reasonably successful in assisting the chronically
ill and the homebound and physically impaired elderly, but assisting the mentally impaired elderly is far more difficult. Often
there is no choice but to turn to the courts. While both tenants
and their families look upon the housing facility as preferable to
any other living arrangement, sponsors of housing for the elderly
face the inescapable problems of gradual conversion of community
housing into homes for the aged, especially for the very old, as
the need for more and more supportive services for these people
change the character of housing for the elderly.

206. Weismehl, R. and Silverstein, D. (1975). An integrated service delivery program for the elderly: Implementing a community
plan. Journal of Jewish Communal Service, 51(3):260-266.

The Jewish Federation of Chicago, and its affiliated agencies,
organized a community gerontological council as a means of confronting basic problems, developing new programs and constructing
new facilities. A study for long range planning was undertaken
and published in 1970. Following this effort an integrated
service delivery system for the elderly was put in operation.
This sytem was to be flexible and compatible with individual needs
of the aged. A package of services was developed and made opera-
tional. Implementation of these services included an outreach
effort, so that the elderly would know about the availability of
the various services, would have easy access to them, and would be
able to decide freely whether or not to use them. Staff were utilized in new roles, and in team approach efforts. Intervention
was based on the idea that needs of the individual take precedence
over any other consideration. Roles and functions of the staff
were defined on the basis of the client's need. Monitoring service delivery was maintained as well to ensure that services would
match the changing needs of Jewish aged.

207. Williams, C. (1984). Reaching isolated older people: I. An
alternative model of day care services. Journal of Gerontological
Social Work, 8(1-2):35-49.

The New Horizons Day Program at the Jewish Home and Infirmary in
Rochester, New York is described. This unique one-day-a-week
adult day program provides social casework and an emphasis on the
participant's life and function. Priority in recruitment to the
program is given to those elderly who are unable to cope with
complex health and welfare systems, and who need supportive social
contacts. Elements of the program are discussed, and case materials are used to illustrate the successful resolution of participants' needs.

208. Williams, C. (1984). Reaching isolated older people: II. An
alternative model of day care services. Journal of Gerontological
Social Work, 8(1-2):51-66.

The services developed to reach isolated old people at the Jewish Home and Infirmary in Rochester, New York are assessed in four
areas: 1) success in reaching the target group; 2) attendance; 3)
length of participation in the program, and 4) resolution of psychosocial and health related problems. Results indicate overall
success with the clientele in all four areas cited. Adult day
services are vital for socially isolated older people. They
should be offered by other nursing homes as a resource for preventing premature institutionalization of those elderly who cannot
maintain themselves in the community without this supportive service.

209. Zoot, V. A. (1980). A program to reduce spiritual depriva-
tion in the nursing home. In Thorson, J. A. and Cook, T. C., Jr.
(Eds.). Spiritual Well-being of the Elderly. Springfield, Ill:
Charles C. Thomas, 195-197.

A Jewish congregation in Skokie, Illinois began a program of
weekly services and celebrations of holidays in 1976. The residents in the facility were quite pleased, especially those among
them who were Jewish. Religious congregations can be effective in
bringing about positive change in long term care.

Issues in Services Delivery

210. Berger, G. (1976). American Jewish communal service 1776-
1976: From traditional self-help to increasing dependence on government support. Jewish Social Studies, 38(3-4):225-246.

Jewish immigrants to America brought with them a historical
tradition of self-help, of "taking care of their own" by the community. This tradition was, and still is, the main factor in the

rise and development of Jewish social welfare agencies for serving the needs of the Jewish community. Helping fellow Jews in times of crisis, and taking responsibility for the welfare of the community, are traits that characterize Jewish welfare philosophy – similar to that of the various Christian denominations. Greater dependence on the government in meeting the welfare needs of a growing population brought a change in the provision of services, as federal policies require a non-sectarian emphasis in social welfare for eligibility to federal support. As a result, Jewish agencies have assumed in the past few decades a quasi governmental status.

211. Blonsky, L. E. (1975). Factors affecting the prospect for survival of a jointly sponsored program for the elderly. Journal of Jewish Communal Service, 52(1):82-90.

New programs on behalf of Jewish aged need commitment by their sponsors to continue with the program beyond the initial funding period. This commitment, however, does not guarantee the survival of the program. Two important factors affecting the likelihood of the continuation of a new program are discussed. These are the autonomy of the program, and the degree to which it has relatively direct access to available community resources. The more these two conditions are met, the more the program will be able to survive. Other factors and models of program development are presented as well. Of these, the jointly sponsored program which utilizes a community action methodology developed as a cooperative program of the Jewish family and Children's Service, along with the Jewish Community Centers Association and the Jewish Center for Aged of St. Louis, is seen by the author as the best for the provision of new services to the elderly. Funding problems, unless resolved in time, can, however, lead to the demise of the program.

212. Cantor, M. H. (1983). Strain among caregivers: A study of experience in the United States. The Gerontologist, 23(6):597-604.

Elderly clients and their primary caregivers served by a major homemaker service in New York City were studied with respect to the strain experienced among them in the process of caregiving. Subjects were marginal income frail elderly, just above the Medicaid eligibility level, who received a 12 week, 12 hours service per week program consisting of homemaker services such as housekeeping, shopping, escort, and personal care. A little above 50 percent of the sample were Jewish elderly, mainly women, of whom close to three-quarters rated themselves as seriously impaired in their functional capacity. The primary caregivers consisted of four groups: spouses (33%); children (36%); other relatives (19%), and friends/neighbors (12%). While, as expected, 70% or more of all caregivers felt "very close" to their care receivers, an inverse correlation appeared between closeness of relationship and ability to get along well. Only half of the children reported that they got along well with their frail elderly parent, compared to 92% of friends and neighbors who got along the best among the four groups of caregivers.

Implications of these and other findings for caregiving and care receiving are discussed, and the need to provide a combination of financial aid, counseling, in-home and respite services to care-givers is stressed as solution to the strains they experience in the process of caregiving.

213. Council of Jewish Federations (1973).   The Jewish aging: Facts for planning. New York Council of Jewish Federations and Welfare Funds, p. 5.

Estimates and projections of the Jewish aged within the national Jewish population are given. A steady rise in percentages is not-ed for each five year cohort since 1971, bringing the proportion of aging to the total Jewish population in excess of 15% by 1991. Persons 65 and over head 21% of Jewish households.   Federation planning must relate especially to this proportion of families since close to half of them report incomes at the poverty level. While the majority of household heads aged 65-69 are native born, 86% of foreign born elderly are in their 80's. The majority of Jewish elderly (87%) live alone or with their spouses. Only 7 percent of Jewish households contain three generations in sharp contrast with previous generations.

214. Dravich, R. B. A comparison of the leisure attitudes of eld-erly Jews and elderly non-Jews. Doctoral dissertation, University of Oregon, 1980. Dissertation Abstracts International, 41(11): 4835A, Order No. 8109674.

The leisure attitudes of elderly Jews and non-Jews in Portland, Oregon, were compared. Subjects were drawn from two community centers and their demographic backgrounds and characteristics as-sessed. Two fifths of the Jewish elderly were foreign born, as opposed to only 5 percent among the non-Jewish elderly in the sam-ple.

Attitudes to leisure were measured by 32 statements covering the subjects' aesthetic, civic, intellectual, mass media, physical, social and spiritual activities. No statistically significant differences were found to exist in the categories of attitudes toward the areas elaborated above, except in social and touristic activities. American born Jewish elderly differed from their Eastern-European born peers in volunteer work and adult education classes.

215. Eran, M. and Jacobson, D. (1976). Expectancy theory prediction of the preference to remain employed or to retire. Journal of Gerontology, 31(5):605–610.

Older workers' choices between continued employment or immediate retirement was assessed using the expectancy theory model of Vroom. Subjects were 290 male workers, 57 to 64 years old, who were facing one of the two choices. Perceived instrumentalities of employment or retirement were measured along valences of 35 outcomes. Results indicated that a person's preference for continued employment or retirement is a function of the difference between the instrumentality of these two alternatives, multiplied by the valence of each outcome. Employers are urged to use additional research for learning about the most appropriate alternatives for their older workers and for preparations to retire.

216. Gelfand, D. E. (1986). Assistance to the New Russian Elderly. The Gerontologist, 26(4):444–449.

A sample of 259 older Russian Jews who recently migrated to the United States and are now living in New York City constituted the respondents to this research. Attitudes toward assistance from various sources were probed by a questionnaire, which was first developed in English, translated into Russian, and retranslated by a third individual to provide a reliability check on the translation process. Group sites used for data collection do not provide a random sample of older Russian Jews, as they do not cater to isolated and poorly educated individuals or those who are averse to using formal services. However, the author believes that the opinions and problems found among the sample are not unrepresentative of the overall situation of older Russian-Jewish immigrants. Reliance on agencies for assistance was cited by 40% of the respondents as being most valuable to the new immigrant, especially initially upon entering the country. Importance of the Russian language newspapers as information sources about day-to-day life in the United States was also cited. The need to develop self-help and support groups is stressed to counter the heavy and continuing reliance by these elderly on agencies for assistance.

217. Gildin, N. B. (1985). Ethical and moral values in homes for the elderly. Journal of Jewish Communal Service, 62(2):178–180.

The Jewish home for the elderly in Connecticut has a philosophy of outreach to the entire Jewish population. Its board of directors maintains policies which enable the resolution of conflicts of interest in ethically sound ways. Outreach services to the community include outpatient physical therapy, day care and congregate feeding programs, and a wide range of other services. Religious programs are designed to stimulate intellectual and ethical interests of the resident population.

218. Ginsberg, Y. (1981). Jewish attitudes toward Black neighbors in Boston and London. Ethnicity, 8(2):206-218.

Interviews with 100 elderly Jews from Boston and with 50 from London revealed a similar attitude toward Black neighbors in racially mixed neighborhoods. While subjects distinguished between "good" and "bad" Blacks, they were generally fearful and perceived Blacks as aggresssive, violent, loud, lazy, and dirty. They also tended to blame blacks for the high crime rate in the city. The similarity of perception and attitudes is interesting considering the fact that the London Jews had Black neighbors of much lower socio-economic status than those in Boston. Since contact with neighbors alone cannot explain the similarity of attitudes, other factors such as cultural heritage may be operating.

219. Goodman, M., Bley, N. and Dye, D. (January, 1974). The adjustment of aged users of leisure programs. American Journal of Orthopsychiatry, 44(1):142-149.

New applicants to a leisure program offered by the St. Louis Jewish Community Center was studied to identify activities that enhance adjustment to leisure programs offered by the Centers. Data were collected on demographic, psychological, and social variables. Patterns of participation varied between male and female respondents with the former reporting less satisfaction with volunteer tasks. Age segregated leisure programs did not meet the needs of a significant proportion of the sample, nor did they enhance adjustment. Matching needs with services requires programming that enables the elderly to benefit from both task oriented and open ended social groups and from both structured and nonstructured activities.

220. Guttmann, D. (1979). Use of informal and formal supports by white ethnic aged. In Gelfand, D. E. and Kutzik, A. J. (Eds.). Ethnicity and Aging, Theory, Research and Policy. New York: Springer Publishing Company, 246-262.

Eight white ethnic groups of elderly and their spokespersons were studied in Washington, D.C. and Baltimore Maryland. The sample comprised of 720 elderly and 180 non-elderly ethnics representing the Estonian, Latvian, Lithuanian, Polish, Hungarian, Jewish, Italian, and Greek communities. The symbolic interaction theory served as the conceptual basis for this research. Attention was focused on the problems and needs of ethnic elderly and on their use of services, both formal and informal, as well as on their reliance on the ethnic community for support. Findings reveal little use of formal services, and raise questions as to the effectiveness of the programs available to the ethnic aged. Theoretical and practical implications of the findings are offered.

221. Guttmann, D. (1973).   Leisure-time activity interests of Jewish aged. The Gerontologist, 13(4):219-223.

Eastern-European and American born and raised elderly Jews have different interest in the activities offered them by community centers due to their cultural upbringing. The former is more oriented toward groups and social clubs, while the latter prefers more individual, or solitary type activities. An understanding of these and other differences among aged within the same religious and ethnic group is important before planning programs for them.

222. Kurland, J. B. and Lipsitz, E. J. (1987).   Rose finally unpacked her belongings. Aging, No. 355, 6-9.

A commercial company in Baltimore, Maryland teamed up with two Jewish communal agencies to provide supportive services to highrise residents in a project funded by the United States Administration on Aging (AOA). The purpose of the grant was to demonstrate how the corporate community and the private, nonprofit agencies could work together to meet the needs of older people. This company had experience in managing housing facilities in which originally well functioning aged were increasingly becoming dependent due to frailty. Vulnerable residents are identified and offered casework services, while small group, and cultural activities are provided by the Jewish Community Center. Outreach efforts have enabled hundreds of frail elderly residents to benefit from these services. The combination of managerial expertize with the philosophy and skills of human services providers is seen as a means for enhancing the independent living of older people in their own homes.

223. Litwin, H. (1986).   The age-integrated community center as a local service base for the elderly: An Israeli analaysis. The Journal of Aging and Judaism, 1(1):22-23.

Community care of informal supports by family and friends is seen as a viable alternative to the more costly institutional care for growing numbers of elderly who survive beyond their eighth decade. Age integrated community centers are viewed as a service framework with good potential for organizing community-based care and for interweaving informal support networks and the statutory social services. There are at present 122 such centers in Israel. Close to half of them sponsor some combination of activities and services for the elderly. These, however, are far from being uniform. Only a minority of these programs can be regarded as bonafide multi-service programs. Models of programming are addressed and traditional Jewish approaches to care of the aged are cited. Lack of services in the other half of the centers surveyed is seen as a result of harsh fiscal and administrative realities. Age integrated community centers in Israel are urged to realize their potential for promoting community-care programming.

224. Mannheim, B. and Rein, J. (1981). Work centrality of different age groups and the wish to discontinue work. International Journal of Aging and Human Development, 13(3):221-232.

Work centrality, age, and the wish to stop working were explored. The sample consisted of 755 males in Israel, who were classified into five occupational categories. The research question to be answered in this paper was whether the factors affecting work centrality in the oldest age group differ from those affecting it in younger age groups. Work centrality was measured by an eight item index. Findings indicate that altogether the variables affecting work centrality in the old age group explain 38 percent of its variance, as against 29 percent in the young group. Age does have an effect on the willingness to stop working. Those willing to stop working have lower level work centrality in all age groups. Job rewards have a moderating effect on this relationship.

225. Maves, P. B. (1988). Religious congregations as healing communities in old age. The Journal of Aging and Judaism, 2(4):237-248.

Spiritual well being is a term which emphasizes the role of religion in a life well lived in the later years. The term was coined by the National Interfaith Coalition on Aging, which defined such well being as the affirmation of life in a relationship with God, self, community and environment that nurtures and celebrates wholeness in spite of the vicissitudes encountered in the process of living. The work of Erik H. Erikson on "ego integrity," as the opposite of despair, is cited as being at the core of the personality, while despair is characterized by mental confusion, inner conflict, self-hatred, and apathy, leading to an inability to cope with the demands of life. Another theoretical approach to wellness used by the author is based on the work of Antonovsky, an Israeli medical sociologist, who is interested in learning what it is that keeps persons from getting sick, or if they get sick what it is that enables them to get well. A "sense of coherence" or a global orientation of confidence that a person has both the resources and finds the challenges worthy of investment of energy is the answer to these questions. Religious congregations can rise to the challenges of modern life, and can set forth a vision of life that is worth living, and they can assist older congregants to reach spiritual well-being in old age.

226. Novick, L. J. (1975). The role of the Rabbi in an Orthodox long-term geriatric hospital. Journal of Jewish Communal Service, 51(4):373-380.

The needs of Jewish geriatric patients in long-term care can be satisfied through the performance of the mitzvot. Patients need both guidance and special conditions in the hospital for the fulfillment of the mitzvot. The rabbi has responsibility for both in this setting. He needs to help patients in the satisfaction of their emotional needs. In the course of his work at the geriatric hospital, the rabbi performs many roles: leading the prayers in the synagogue; giving opportunities for all patients to take part in the blessing of removal of the Torah scroll from the ark; teaching patients about Judaism; involving patients in planning and decision making with regard to the religious services and observances of the Sabbath and High Holy Days, and serving as therapist in small-group sessions. Understanding the needs of geriatric patients of the staff members and collaboration with other professionals and of the hospital at large, are major requirements for the successful fulfillment of this role.

227. Penning, M. J. and Chappell, N. L. (1987). Ethnicity and informal supports among older adults. Journal of Aging Studies,1 (2):145-160.

Five ethnic groups residing in Winnipeg, Manitoba in Canada, were compared in terms of availability of support, their interactions, satisfactions, exchanges of assistance and relationships with confidants. Data were derived from a sample of 400 recipients and 400 non-recipients of home care, stratified by age, sex, and region, 65 years old and older, who were randomly selected and interviewed in 1980. Findings revealed certain similarities among the groups in number of friends who were available for help. Greater access to assistance was noted among the French and German groups, as opposed to the Jewish, British, and other ethnic groups. Implications of these findings for the conceptualization of patterns of ethnic variance in use of informal networks of support are discussed.

228. Prager, E. and Shnit, D. (1985–86). Organizational environments and care outcome decisions for elderly clientele: A view
from Israel. Administration in Social Work, 9(4):49–61.

An exploratory study of care outcome decisions was conducted
with 68 aged clients. Social workers in Agency Type A saw themselves as being directly responsible for the decision on relocation, despite a participative ideology which left such decisions
to the internal older person's unit committee. Workers in agency
Type B, which was guided by a nonparticipative orientation, viewed
themselves as being at a greater reach from the locus of formal
decision making and as being more involved as data collectors and
processors. Based on these results the authors hypothesized that
in Israel participative and nonparticipative structures lead to
significantly different care outcomes for elderly clientele.

229. Rosenzweig, N. (1975).   Some differences between elderly
people who use community resources and those who do not. Journal
of the American Geriatrics Society, 23(5):224–233.

A 442 item questionnaire about family background, current
status, personal data, attitudes, interests and self-concept was
administered to 90 subjects divided by their use or nonuse of
community resources to three equal sized groups. Those who lived
alone and or with their families were better educated, were more
successful financially, obtained more satisfaction from their
work, had closer family ties but were also more threatened by illness than their counterparts who relied more on community resources offered by the Jewish Community Center. These differences
among the three groups need to be taken into consideration by
planners of services for the aged.

230. Rubin, B. (1977). The role of the community center in meeting the health needs of the aged: An overview, Journal of Jewish
Communal Service, 54(1):32–38.

A description of present and projected prevention health programs in community centers is presented. Such programs can preserve the happiness and dignity of Jewish aged, are less costly
then nursing home care, and may be useful in preventing or delay-
ing custodial care of the frail, isolated and depressed elderly.

231. Salamon, M. J. (1988).   Jewish patients in nursing homes
under non-Jewish auspices: Some personal observations.   The
Journal of Aging and Judaism, 2(3):196-200.

The number of nursing home residents in the United States has
increased threefold during the past two decades.   It is continuing
to rise even more in coming years.   Nursing home beds cannot keep
pace with this increase, especially in Jewish sponsored facilities, as the number of Jewish aged in need of nursng home care is
on the rise.   There are many reasons why frail Jewish elderly
cannot be cared for in their own homes.   These are elaborated by
the author.   Nursing home care is not always a sign of abandonment
of the elderly by their families, as the decision to placement is
a heart rending one for all involved.   The issue of providing a
Jewish environment for the sick parent who has to move to a
nursing home is complicated by economic and other factors and by
the inavailability of nursing homes under Jewish auspices.   Non-
Jewish facilities can help their Jewish aged residents and their
families by creating a Jewish atmosphere on their premises.   This
includes the provision of kosher foods, Jewish prayer services and
family visitation as needed.

232. Schwamm, J. (1983).   Housing well-elderly: A case study and
critique of planning in an intermediate Jewish community.   Journal
of Jewish Communal Service, 59(4):340-349.

The planning process used in an intermediate Jewish community
for housing the well-elderly is described.   A basic assumption
underlying planning is that the match between the elderly client
and his needs and between the organizational context affecting
services should be maintained.   A rational model of planning is
presented.   Ten individuals were identified as key participants in
planning the housing.   Based on various reports goals were developed by staff.   These included the following: (1) to provide
housing for senior citizens who need and want housing in a Jewish
environment; (2) to maintain and foster the independence of tenants, and (3) to create a Jewish atmosphere in the apartment
house.   There were no Jewish well-elderly involved in the process
of planning.   Therefore many questions were either not raised or
given only lipservice...

233. Shwayder-Hughes, M. L.   The impact of institutionalization
upon the Jewish aged: A comparative approach, Doctoral dissertation, University of Colorado at Boulder, 1979. Dissertation Abstracts International, 40(4): 2298-A, Order No. 7923286.

Using a symbolic interactionist perspective, this study compared
36 residents in an apartment complex for the aged with 36 residents in a home for the aged.   A scale of anomie and alienation
was derived by utilizing factor analysis. Institutionalization was

found to be related to the age of the individual and to his/her child's upward mobility. Socially induced problems are expressed in a sense of alienation among institutionalized elderly. Being a member of a stigmatized group in a social setting that infantiliz-es the aged is detrimental to the mental health of the aging. Alteration of the social conditions, such as encouragement of in-dependence, will allow individuals to reject stigmatization and will improve their self-concept.

234. Warach, B. (1982). Frontiers of service to the aging. Jour-nal of Jewish Communal Service, 59(1):26-34.

The challenges lying ahead for Jewish communities in America to meet the needs of a vastly increased elderly Jewish population are described. The need to develop comprehensive services based on close coordination between health agencies, community centers, and other institutions is stressed. Six frontiers in communal ser-vices for the aged are cited: (1) a commitment to a program of advocacy in the public area on behalf of the elderly; (2) renewal of a planning effort by agencies to assess the status of the eld-erly and to develop new programs; (3) organizing an educational program for the Jewish community on "growing older;" (4) adequate provision of social work services for the elderly under Jewish communal auspice; (5) development of comprehensive diagnosis, casemanagement, coordinated home care, and protective services for the chronically disabled, and (6) development of home care ser-vices for the impaired elderly.

235. Warach, B. (1977). Matching services and activities to meet the needs of older people. Journal of Jewish Communal Services, 53(4):250-259.

The need to provide comprehensive services to the elderly along a continuum of care requires cooperative efforts by the govern-ment, the larger community, and by the Jewish Communal and volun-tary organizations. Each Jewish community is requested to assess the problems of its aged, to determine priorities, to develop strategies for mobilization of resources, and to assure access to services by Jewish aged. Benefits and entitlements for institu-tional, health, and housing care are enumerated by Title, and guidelines for program planning are offered. In light of the ever increasing size of the aged within the total Jewish population, communities must be prepared to provide services ranging from the intact to the physically disabled and mentally impaired aging.

236. Warach, B. (1975). Decentralization, community control, and citizen participation in the provision of services for the Jewish aged. Journal of Jewish Communal Service, 51(4):366-372.

This article provides a review of the Jewish Association for Services to the Aged in New York (JASA). Organized in the late sixties by the Federation of Jewish Philanthropies of New York, JASA was established to develop and provide comprehensive services for the care of Jewish aged in the community. It has completed numerous building programs, neighborhood-based community service centers and group service programs. The agency has been unable to open facilities for the mentally impaired elderly, as resistance to such a facility came from all directions, including other Jewish communities. Lessons learned from the six years in which JASA has grown to a large, decentralized and diverse agency are summarized. The need to gain the sanction of local communities for expansion of agency facilities and programs is stressed.

237. Watson, W. H. (1979). Resistances to naturalistic observation in a geriatric setting. International Journal of Aging and Human Development, 10(1):35-45.

A stationary camera with an audio-video taping system was used to view staff initiated touching among the Jewish residents of a home for the aged. Systematic comparisons were made in relation to naturalistic variations among the subjects by such variables as physical appearances, sex, age, and social statuses of interaction partners. Resistance to naturalistic observation in geriatric settings by staff center around ethical and methodological issues. These are discussed at length by the author.

238. Wish, F. (1980). Day care: Its value for the older adult and his family. Journal of Jewish Communal Service, 57(2):174-180.

Day care services to older adults were initially developed in the 1940s by psychiatric day hospitals. Today there are three distinct types of day care centers: 1) those in senior centers that deal primarily with persons who are in relatively good health; 2) those that provide a protective environment to persons with limited functional capacity, and 3) day care centers for the severely handicapped, who need health care, rehabilitation services and support. An emerging day care program is geared to the mentally impaired elderly. Common to all types of day care centers for older adults is that they emphasize social and health programming. These services benefit the elderly and their families.

6 Education for Working with Jewish Elderly

Gerontological and Geriatric Education

239. Berman, R. U. (1981). A Judaic journey creates communication; in-service education of staff of a Jewish home for the aged. Journal of Jewish Communal Service, 58(1):61–66.

The importance of religion in late life has been recognized by gerontologists. Studies done in this area of life have shown a significant correlation between life satisfaction and religious activity. Religious education of the staff is necessary to increase their knowledge of customs and traditions and for facilitating greater communication between employees and residents. A training program for staff, initially requested by the licensed practical nurses, is described. Content included knowledge of Jewish holidays and festivals; attitudes to major social issues, and to important historical events such as the Holocaust, and the establishment of the State of Israel. The training program was found to be helpful in destroying prejudices, myths, and stereotypes.

240. Blech, B. (1976–77). Judaism and gerontology. Tradition: A Journal of Orthodox Thought, 16:65–78.

The tremendous difference in attitude to the aged between the Biblical ideal and contemporary reality is dealt with in this article. Ageism or societal prejudice against the aged is rapidly being recognized as a serious problem today. Many elderly people perceive their longevity as a curse, rather than a blessing. The Bible, on the other hand, saw in long life a reward for the fulfillment of the Commandments. The Talmud believes that the old are not beyond help. They are still capable of personal growth. Companionship, sex, as a "pleasure need," and remarriage after the loss of the spouse, are all Biblical requirements. Their purpose is to maintain good physical and mental health among the aged.

241. Chaiklin, H. and Lowenstein, A. (1982). Social work training to meet the needs of the aged in Israel. Gerontology and Geriatric Education, 2(3):243-248.

The 1978 estimate of the Jewish population in Israel included 9.4 percent elderly aged 65 years old and older. Education in social work for serving this segment of the population follows similar lines to those given in the English speaking countries and is based on the social and cultural aspects of the aged; on the organization of services for the aged, and on organization of the professional education. The three aspects of education in social gerontology are elaborated by the authors. At the time this article was written there were two schools, one in Tel Aviv and the other in Haifa that offered concentrations in aging. These served to generate new workers and new programs and services for the aged in Israel.

242. Cibulski, O. and Bergman, S. (1981). Mutuality of learning between the old and the young: A case study in Israel. Ageing and Society, 1(2):247-262.

The knowledge of old people, their past and present teaching-learning experiences with children, and their readiness to teach children in the future were explored. Subjects included 76 old people from three cultural groups in Israel, of whom 44 were women over 60, and 32 men over 65. They were chosen purposively in order to examine the effects of culture on intergenerational relationships. A number of different types of knowledge was identified by the researchers as applicable to the sample. These included occupational skills, personal experience, religious, and general knowledge. Positive experiences in teaching children were noted by those aged who perceived themselves as competent, who had frequent contacts with school age children, and who were prepared to teach children in the future, especially about family tradition. Teaching children provides an opportunity to the old to enhance their self-esteem and to gain satisfaction from the mutuality of sharing the teaching-learning experience with the young.

243. Galinsky, D. (1987). Geriatrics in the framework of University-based community medicine. Israel Journal of Medical Sciences, 23(9-10):136-138.

The geriatric service in the Negev region of Israel was launched in 1974 to provide care for this region's culturally varied population. Its main purpose was to keep this aged population in their own homes as long as possible. The service relies on the cooperation and collaboration of both public and governmental agencies in health care provision. Interaction by the staff of

these agencies allow ongoing assessment of patients by a multidisciplinary team and flexible shifting to services as per the
individual need of the patient. The teaching program at the
Recanati School of Community Health professions is described. All
the instructors in this program are themselves involved in services for the elderly. Research is community oriented and deals
with the special problems of the elderly in the Negev.

244. Galinsky, D. (1985). Ten years' experience teaching geriatric medicine. Israel Journal of Medical Sciences, 21:249-253.

Using the facilities of the Department of Geriatrics at the
Soroka Medical Center in Beer-Sheva, Israel, the faculty of Health
Sciences of the Ben-Gurion University of the Negev has developed a
comprehensive curriculum in geriatric medicine for medical, nursing and physiotherapy schools. Subjects taught include observation, communication, multidisciplinary teamwork, biology, physical
examination, common clinical problems, and management of bedridden
patients. This educational package is aimed at the eradication of
stigma associated with work in geriatric services. The need for
new geriatrics departments, new health care policies, and recognition of the need to provide comprehensive services for the aged
are discussed.

245. Galinsky, D., Cohen, R., Schneirman, C., Gelper,Y. and Nir,
Z. (1983). A programme in undergraduate geriatric education: The
Beer Sheva experiment. Medical Education, 17:100-104.

A programme developed at the Beer Sheva medical school to deal
with the health-related problems of the aged is described. This
programme started in 1974 when the medical school was established.
During their six years of training as primary care doctors, students are introduced to elderly patients and continue this exposure in varying degrees throughout the curriculum. Students begin
their studies with a positive attitude toward the elderly. The
early clinical training reinforces this trend. Students need
positive role models to maintain their interest in working with
the elderly. Consequently both hospital and community-based physicians need to undertake such roles. This request is directed
especially to family doctors working in the established community
clinics, as these are the main providers of health care for the
elderly. The innovative educational programme at Beer Sheva's
medical school together with a modified health care clinic will,
as hoped by the authors, lead to the introduction of a new kind of
doctor to meet the needs of people in the Negev.

246. Glanz, D.   (1985).   Higher education and retirement: The Israeli experience. Educational Gerontology, 11(2-3):101-111.

The development, organization, and status of educational programs for retired persons in three Israeli universities are described. Data covering the past five years prior to this study highlight the participants' backgrounds, their interest in higher education, motivation to study and their social relationship with other students. Literature on higher education for retired persons cited, and the relevance of this Israeli experience to other countries discussed.

247. Glanz, D. (1984). Aging and education in Israel: A sociological perspective. Educational Gerontology, 10(3):245-267.

The social meaning of education for the aged in Israel is presented along with the educational frameworks and opportunities available to persons 60 years old and older. Education serves a dual purpose: it enhances individual knowledge, and provides a readily available avenue for meaningful use of time. Elderly students acquire social status commonly reserved for the young, and consequently, an increased sense of self-esteem. Changes in the structure of Israeli society are analyzed and linked to the specifics of the aging process in the country.

248. Glanz, D. and Tabori, E. (1985). Higher education and retirement: The Israeli experience. Educational Gerontology, 1 (2-3):101-111.

Higher education for retired persons offered by three Israeli universities is reviewed. Each program's development organization, and current status is described. Data pertaining to participants socioeconomic background, their motivations and interest in the program are presented. The Israeli experience in teaching retired persons via the "Open Door College," which won the Lapid Prize by Israeli National Association for Adult Education, is offered as potentially relevant for retired persons in other countries.

249. Hirschfeld, M. (1984). "Ideology," change, and aging education. Gerontology and Geriatrics Education, 4(3):3-13.

The dramatic increase in the number of the old population in Israel is illustrated by statistics which indicate that the aged 65 years and over grew more than seven times in 40 years of the Jewish state's existence. A large proportion of these people is afflicted with chronic diseases and with functional disabilities and need a wide variety of services, and especially long term

care. Professional education of nurses must confront these conditions. Denial of the topic will not solve the problem. A
second order change is advocated meaning a different way of
looking at the problem and dealing with it. The process leading
to the envisioned change is described and an ideology is presented
along with educational programs within this conceptual frame.

**250. Kaye, L. W. (1986). Educating our children about growing
older: A challenge to Jewish education. The Journal of Aging and
Judaism, 1(1):6–21.**

A rationale and strategy for teaching young people about growing
older are offered in the context of the Jewish system of education. Learning about aging is viewed in broad terms as a continuing functional responsibility throughout the learner's life cycle.
The rationale presented relies on the social, economic, and psychological implications of a rapidly growing elderly population.
The need to devise ways in which the necessary resources to meet
the challenges of an aging society will be secured is stressed.
Jewish tradition in care of the aged is cited as another aspect of
the rationale, albeit with some reservations. The relevant types
of gerontological content envisioned by the author include Jewish
attitudes toward the aged, synagogue and social programming, and a
generic curriculum of human development and aging.

**251. Kravitz, L. (1988). Old age and the Midrash: A thoughtful
introduction. The Journal of Aging and Judaism, 2(3):158–161.**

Midrash is the rabbinic interpretation of Scripture. The term
may refer either to the methods of investigation and exposition of
the Biblical text or to the literature thereby created by a particular group of scholars, living in the main in Palestine from
the first to the tenth century of the present era. Midrashic
literature offers insights on the human condition, on life in the
present and direction for the future. Since aging is a human
condition, old age is treated in the Midrash. The story of
Abraham before and after Sarah's death illuminates Midrashic
treatment of old age. It was the death of Sarah, his beloved
wife, not the passage of the years, that made Abraham old.
A sudden onset of "old age" in the surviving spouse is often
related to the death of a beloved mate. Old age leaps upon a man
be anxiety, by vexation in the raising of children, by a malevo-
lent wife, and by fear induced by wars. Aging can be retarded by
shielding a loved one from the above characteristics of premature
aging. Nurturing and caring are seen as antidotes to the stresses
and anxieties of modern life. Implications of the Midrash for
Jewish communal life, for the education of clergy, and for
programs to serving the aged are presented.

252. Laor, U. (Winter, 1985). Israel seeks to integrate aging into school curricula. Ageing International, 12(4):5.

In this brief report the director of the Association for the
Planning and Development of Services for the Aged in Israel
(ESHEL) describes a special effort undertaken by the above organization to encourage the study of aging throughout the Israeli
educational system. The "gerontologization" of school curricula
implies a need to train leaders with a skill to work within the
schools. Retired teachers can form the spearhead of this effort.
Educational materials for elementary and for high school students,
grants for university education of teachers, and closer links with
associations serving the aged are among the highlights of this
report.

253. Shine, M. and Steitz, J. A. (1988). Teachings of Judaism on
death: A celebration of life. The Journal of Aging and Judaism,
2(3):191-195.

Two aspects of Judaims that relate to death and dying are
presented. The first describes aging as a natural process and
dying as a personal crisis. The second explains a traditional
Jewish role for the bereaved. In Judaism the respect and joy of
life includes death, as the final aspect of life. In the Jewish
tradition the dying person is helped to accept approaching death,
while the mourners are guided tenderly how to face the death of a
loved one. The year of mourning is organized in such a way as to
help the mourners to gradually return to normal life. There are
the concurrent periods of three days of deep grief following death
and burial, seven days of mourning held at the home of the de-
ceased, or the shivah, 30 days of gradual readjustment, and 12
months of remembrance and healing. The anniversary of the death
of a relative, or the yahrzeit, is a recognized annual event.
Judaism emphasizes respect for the dying and the dead. A last
minute vidui, or deathbed confession, represents the final reconciliation between self and God. Death proves that our time on
earth is limited. It is the final stage of growth. Judaism views
death as both a personal crisis and as a communal event, in which
the community provides for the emotional needs of the mourner.

Training and Programming for Work with Jewish Aged

254. Beaver, M. L. and Elias, B. (1980). Enhancing the well-being
of the marginal elderly through art appreciation. Conference
Paper, 16p. Paper presented at the Annual scientific meeting of
the Gerontological Society (33rd, San Diego, CA, November 21-25,
1980). Journal Announcement:RIEJU L81.

A ten week experimental class in painting for older adults at
the Jewish Community Center is described. Subjects were nineteen
relatively isolated persons, aged 65-84 years, who met for 2-hour

weekly sessions. Discussion centers on this socially and personally enriching experience for the participants. Instructional
methods, and various techniques for leading such groups are provided. Changes in student behavior, evaluation of the class, and
plans for the future are also presented.

**255. Becker, R. G. (1976).   The physician assistant in geriatric
long-term care. The Gerontologist, 16(4):318–321.**

Physician assistants are a new "breed" of health care professionals in geriatrics. Their functions are to serve as extensions
to the physicians and to perform relatively simple procedures vis-
a-vis the patient. The author's experience at the Jewish Institute for Geriatric Care is described using 71 physician assistant
students as the base for his analysis.

**256. Bergman, R. and Golander, H. (1982).   Evaluation of care for
the aged: A multipurpose guide. Journal of Advanced Nursing, 7
(2):230–210.**

The need to evaluate quality of care of the aged, who are often
dependent on caregivers for many years is stressed. A tool prepared by an interdisciplinary workgroup taps six domains in evaluating care: physical environment, psychosocial environment, basic
personal care, health care, family involvement and manpower. One
of the advantages of this tool is that it can be used by a large
array of lay and professional persons, including clients and families in selecting placements for care.
A set of recommendations for action by government and other voluntary agencies involved in the care of the aged is offered for
implementation in service, for teaching and for research.

**257. Cohen, C. J. (1978).   Supervision of senior citizen craft
teachers: Goals and practice. Journal of Jewish Communal Service, 55(2):105–111..**

The primary goals of most crafts programs have been socialization, social interaction and the formation of group identity.
These, while legitimate, may neglect to see the senior citizen as
a learner with a need for some tangible accomplishment. The importance of learning something new, to struggle with the material
and with the self, to proceed from ignorance to hope, and to tri-
umph is at the heart of this innovative program. Designed for retired housewives, and for blue collar workers with lots of ability
in handicrafts but with limited experience in teaching others, the
program and its supervision enable participants to gain such
skills at the Kings Bay YM-YWHA. Organization of the classroom,
areas of supervision, and specific techniques are enumerated, and
learning opportunities for senior members are cited.

258. Friedman, D. A. (1987).   The mitzvah model: A therapeutic resource for the institutionalized aged.   The Journal of Aging and Judaism, 1(2):96-108.

Jewish religious obligation of performing the commandments or Mitzvot, can provide older institutionalized people means to living in a sense of dignity and self-esteem. They are seen by the author as potential measures for ameliorating feelings of worthlessness, which are so pervasive among old persons who live in institutions. The "mitzvah model" is accessible even to the frail, and the impaired older person, as it allows individual variations in its use. Moreover, performance of the Mitzvot can lead to honor, importance and success within the Jewish social world of the institution and to fill the time with meaningful acts and activities, as well as with social roles that are valued in such a community. While the Halachic literature contains allowances for frailty, it does not provide direct answers to the special needs of the very old and frail Jews in institutions. In the nursing home setting there is a need for a flexible, easily adaptable model of Mitzvot, one which takes into account the frailties of the residents and the obstacles that are present in fulfilling religious obligations. Mitzvot can be used not only creatively and flexibly, but therapeutically as well. Illustrations for adapting religious obligations to nursing home residents therapeutically, by using language and by actual teaching, are offered along with the message that adaptive observance is not a compromise, nor is it inferior to the "real" one.

259. Furchtgott, A. K. (1981-1982).   A support group of elderly Russian immigrants.   Journal of Jewish Communal Service, 58(3): 231-238.

The Jewish Family Service in Detroit maintains a program of resettlement for Soviet immigrants whose main clientele is the elderly. The losses suffered by these people in the their move to the United States, and the difficulties faced by them in forming and creating a new life, brought a recognition by the staff that a support group comprised of the most needy among the immigrants would help the most isolated, depressed and troubled individuals in adjusting themselves to life in the community. Activities conducted by this support group are presented along with the rationale and methodology of forming such groups. Themes and issues discussed at the meetings enable the participants to share their experiences in dealing with the authorities, to come to terms with past grievances and to learn about ways to lessen members' severe isolation.

260. Harpaz, I. and Kremer, Y. (1981). Determinants of continued and discontinued participation in pre-retirement training: An Israeli case study. Journal of Occupational Psychology, 54:213-220.

Two groups of older workers in five industrial and public service organizations were compared as to their rate of attendance at the first training program in Israel prior to retirement. The purpose of the study was to identify the differences in the characteristics of those who continued versus those who did not in the program. Findings indicated that occupational level, contact with grandchildren, attitude towards pre-retirement training, and enjoyment of the present job were the best explanatory and discriminating variables in predicting participation or non-participation in pre-retirement training programs. The authors claim that these findings may be useful for reaching out to workers who are reluctant to participate in such training.

261. Joseph, S. K. (1988). Proposal for a ceremony for retirement. The Journal of Aging and Judaism, 2(3):180-186.

Despite the great wealth of wisdom found in Jewish sources of learning, one area was not mentioned by the sages-retirement, as it was a foreign concept for them. Life expectancy today, as opposed to Biblical times enables millions to look forward to decades in which they will be elders, with grey hair, and with strength. Retirement is not the end of life, rather the beginning of a new phase in it today. Therefore it should be celebrated by a special ceremony in the synagogue, like Bar-Mitzvah, Confirmation, or marriage.

A creative ceremony for retirement that could be inserted in a regular Shabbat service is elaborated, with readings by the Rabbi, the congregation, and the retiree.

262. Kaminsky, M. (1985). The arts and social work: Writing and reminiscing in old age: Voices from within the process. Journal of Gerontological Social Work.

The importance of writing in old age is discussed in poetic terms using illustrations from writings done by elderly people. The writer attempts to bring the whole soul into activity. Teaching old people to write as writers do requires time and repeated attempts to capture a feeling. A writers' workshop brings into play a wide range of emotional and intellectual processes that have adaptive value in old age. Members who participated in such a workshop summed up their experiences by stating that it enabled them: (1) to continue learning; (2) to draw upon unused skills, experience, knowledge; to put themselves to use; (3) to resume an interest of their youth; (4) to satisfy their need for continued accomplishments; (5) to communicate with themselves and to explore

their inner worlds; (6) to communicate with others by making contacts with people who have suffered and struggled like themselves;
(7) to become more involved with their present daily lives in
order to enrich them by this activity; (8) to find meaning in
suffering; (9) to imagine, create, play with words, images, ideas
and feelings; (10) to review their lives, and (11) to transmit
their life experience to those who come after them.

**263. Kaye, L. W. and Monk, A. (1987). Gerontological careers and
workplace priorities: Expectations and experiences of Jewish professionals. The Journal of Aging and Judaism, 2(2):67–84.**

Recent graduates of a major college of religious instruction
were surveyed. The aim was to learn of career preparation, personal expectations, and workplace experience in the area of
services to the elderly. The majority of the 216 subjects were
practicing rabbis. Jewish communal workers, educators, and
cantors constituted the rest of the sample. Respondents were the
least prepared to work with the elderly. Consequently, the vast
majority of them were convinced that they needed training in the
subjects of death and dying, human relations, gerontological
counseling, and developmental psychology. Rabbis stood out in
this study as a group which supported an "age irrelevant"
philosophy in their work within the synagogue. Jewish communal
workers, on the other hand, saw their work with the elderly as
greatly significant.

**264. Kurland, J. (1987). Training program for building managers
serving the elderly: A partnership delivers. Journal of Jewish
Communal Service, 64(2):179–185.**

A cooperative venture between a private for-profit management
company and a voluntary non-profit social agency is described in
three parts. The first part traces the history of the agency's
efforts in which the training program was developed. A detailed
description of the training course itself is presented next, while
an evaluation of the experience and the results of this cooperation constitute the third part of this paper. A sense of partnership has been developed between agency staff and building managers
the author states. Encouraged with the results, the agency looks
at this work as a prototype that can serve as a model for other
state and national collaborative ventures in training building
managers serving the elderly.

265. Linzer, N. (1987).   Resolving ethical dilemmas in the Jewish Community Center.   Journal of Jewish Communal Service, 64(2):145–155.

This article continues a discussion on identifying and resolving ethical dilemmas in Jewish communal service, which were originally presented in the 1986 issue of this journal.   Three cases from a Federation, a Jewish family service, and a senior adult vocation center were analyzed according to the theoretical base.   Continued exploration of those ideas and the ideological issues confronting the Jewish community center field are followed by a discussion of two cases of ethical dilemmas.   The Center field in the last decade has seen great changes in staffing, programming and policy development.   Today a plethora of Jewish communal service workers are employed by the Centers.   Both Jewish and general social work ethics constitute the Centers' ideology.   The dual emphasis on the ethical responsibility of the professionals often result in ethical dilemmas, for there is always a potential for value and ethical conflict when these two systems of thought are juxtaposed.

266. Macarov, D. (1987).   Social work with the aged: Some future projections.   Journal of Social Work and Policy in Israel, 1(1):7–24.

Changes awaiting social workers now entering the profession during their future careers will include an increased life expectancy, and consequently an ever-growing demand for help at home, in institutions and in the community.   Expected demographic changes will lead to a fast-growing and a large elderly population, while more and more women who enter the labor force will not be available to provide care for their frail parents.   Thus social workers will have to develop new foci, new knowledge, and new methods of practice to deal with these changes.   Since many of the present social work services will be offered by volunteers and by paraprofessionals, social workers will find themselves largely in supervisory, consultative, and executive positions.

267. Mecklenburger, R. (1987).   The privilege of worrying: A modern midrash on Genesis.   The Journal of Aging and Judaism, 2(2):108–111.

Originally presented as a Torah commentary before the author's congregation, this article maintains that we are tested in each generation the same way Abraham and Isaac were.   What modern day parents need to learn is not how to worry about their children, for worrying means caring.   Rather, how to differentiate between healthy concern, which is based on love and fosters growth, and unhealthy worry, and nudging, which can stunt personal development.   Obligations of familial love flow both ways across the generational divide.   Those who have loved ones to care for and to

worry about, and those whose loved ones worry about them are the
blessed ones. Taking on the challenges that life brings gives
meaning to our existence.

**268. Olitzky, K. M. (1988). Old age as the Sabbatical transforma-
tion of life: A model for all faiths. The Journal of Aging and
Judaism, 2(4):210-220.**

This article is based on a presentation the author made at the
Aging Institute at the College of Mt. St. Joseph in Cincinnati,
Ohio, on the subject of interfaith ministry to the aged. Its
message is not to talk about interfaith projects, but to talk in-
stead about living and working together in the same community, as
neighbors and friends. The author argues that a sabbatical transformation of life in old age is a spiritual one. It can transform
our lives and climax in old age - reaching its peak in old age.
As on the Sabbath, in old age we are relieved of certain obligations. The Sabbath literally moves us from one level of consciousness to another. In old age we move from one stage to the
next, and it is an enriching experience. Faith, spirituality and
a life of fulfilling good deeds grow with us as we grow older -
provided that we nurture them in the course of the life cycle.
Spirituality can be reached by the mitzvot. It is therefore the
responsibility of the Jewish spiritual leaders to do the nurturing
with the members, including the old, of his congregation. To lead
a spiritual life means, according to the author, to live a life in
the study of the Torah, and to perform good deeds. As the Sabbath
is the anchor of the week, which allows one to taste a glimpse of
life with a vision and meaning, so is old age that prepares us for
eternity. In old age we have to transform our creative energies
into spiritual ones to sustain the soul more than the body.

**269. Olitzky, K. M. (1988). Interfaith challenges in working with
older adults in communities of different faiths: Two case studies. The Journal of Aging and Judaism, 2(4):249-256.**

Case studies are offered to illustrate two different religious
perspectives in their approach to interfaith programs in a religious school. The purpose is to raise concern for the elderly and
to help bridge the gap between Jews and non-Jews. Case number one
is actually two cases: one in a secular nursing home and the
other in a retirement community. These cases are presented and
analyzed by a geriatric social worker who is active in the Episco-
palian Church, and by a Jewish administrator and teacher of social
work. The problems presented in both cases seem on their surface
as being connected to religion. The solutions offered, however,
are in line with established values of the social work profession.

270. Olitzky, K. M. (1987). Parashat Noah, Genesis 6:9-11:32: A practical response. The Journal of Aging and Judaism, 2(2):123-127.

The Biblical character of Noah is presented as a role model for today's rapidly increasing elderly population. This hero of the Bible was 600 years old when God unleashed the flood, and in his hands the destiny of the world was entrusted. Noah is described as blameless in his age, someone who has walked with God. He had the care and the respect of his children, and the strength of a young man even in his old age. Why did God choose an elder to save the world? According to the Bratzlaver Rebbe: "Old men bring stability to Israel and good counsel to the people." Since Noah was a leader and a teacher he serves as a paradigm for the elderly and a source of inspiration for the young as well.

271. Olitzky, K. M. (1985). Synagogue: A new concept for a new age. Journal of Jewish Communal Service, 62(1):8-10.

The synagogue's unique role in educating both young and old is raised and discussed. Being a pluralistic institute, the synagogue is the reflection of the Jewish spiritual self. Therefore, it cannot be singular in its religious and social service. There is a need to educate the lay leadership to be sensitive to the changing needs of the congregation, and to the beneficial effects of having a ministerial care team taking care for those needs. Programming, education, and ministry provide challenges, rather than problems, the author states. The synagogue could become the center of the Jewish Community by using creative approaches in building and program utilization, and by reaching out to populations that need a supportive environment, such as the elderly.

Intergenerational Contacts

272. Bayer, S. and Bayer, E. (1975). You and your aging parent: A laboratory approach. Journal of Jewish Communal Service, 52(2): 174-181.

In order to improve the relationships between senior adult parents and their adult children, a program of experiential and experimental learning was offered by the Senior Adult Department of the Jewish Community Center in Pittsburgh. The program focused on the needs of the adult child. It was designed to sensitize the participants to the needs of older parents; to help them express feelings, and to share experiences in dealing with such feelings. A planning group was put into operation of the program along with the professional group workers of the Center. The dual approach yielded considerable success in easing the tensions between adult children and their parents. The method also allowed participants to accomplish their task. Based on this success, a second group came to the Center not to plan but to participate in this program.

273. Becker, D. G. (1976). Grandparents rediscovered. Journal of Jewish Communal Services, 53(3):240–248.

Discussion on grandparents by students are seen as exciting educational tools in gerontology courses. They can unlock feelings and attitudes towards the old, and can help students to gain a better understanding of the aging process. These in turn may be utilized in professional work with elderly clients. A course held under the auspices of the Israel Ministry of Social Welfare for 18 social workers assigned to work with the aged in Tel Aviv is described. Course content focused on the nature of the aging process, on the needs of the aged, and on the existing policies and services to deal with the needs of the aged. Practice and skill development methods were also addressed in this course.

274. Berman, R. and Geis, E. (1975). Intergenerational contact: Theological and social insights. Religious Education, 70:661–675.

Sixteen single Roman Catholic college students in New York state made contacts with the residents at Riverdale Hebrew Home for the Aged. The theological and social analysis of the students' anticipation of their own aging, acceptance or rejection of old age, feelings about institutionalized care, discovery of the elderly, and concentration on a death and dying course is presented. Implications of the findings for future study are drawn.

275. Berman, R. U. and Samuels, B. W. (1980). An adventure in learning: Hebrew for home residents. Journal of Jewish Communal Service, 56(4):361–365.

Study of the Torah provides two basic educational principles; first that it should not be viewed as distinct from the inner content of life; and second, that education should be a life-long commitment and obligation. Based on this premise, a model of an effective Hebrew language program at the Hebrew Home for the Aged in Riverdale, New York was introduced. The background of the aged students, the educational considerations in teaching the very old, the methodology employed, and implications of the program for expanding educational opportunities are discussed. Institutionalized aged are willing to study when properly motivated. There is a need to create an educational environment which would be conducive for the residents to involve themselves in such pursuits. Emphasis should be placed on participation of each member, rather than on evaluation of performance. There is also a need to provide positive reinforcement and to help students feel at ease in this learning process.

276. Cottle, T. (1977). The smell of time: Portraits of the aging. Moment, 3(4):29-38.

The author's work with poor Jewish families, and among them many elderly with whom he has conversed hundreds of hours, is described. Four vignettes of aged Jewish individuals are drawn. Their stories and experiences are presented with lots of feeling. There is a sincere attempt to capture the essence of time for them - and for the author as well.

277. Forman, B. I. (1981). Toward an age-blind society. Reconstructionist, XLVI:20-25.

Among the innovative programs offered by communal agencies to alleviate the plight of the aged the author cites Homecrest House in Silver Spring, Maryland. Residents of this Jewish home, most of them 80 years old and older, enjoy independent living and a wide variety of cultural activities. They are allowed to have their own House Council and to take an active part in running their own affairs. Old people should be looked at and perceived by Americans as just like any other people, with a right to work, and a right to receive assistance when they can no longer take care of themselves. Stereotypes of aging need to be eliminated and mandatory retirement should be outlawed.

278. Isaacs, L. W. (1987). Intergeneration families. The Journal of Aging and Judaism, 2(2):84-93.

Modern grandparenthood is the result of demographic and sociological changes of the last few decades. Today there are more grandparents because people live longer. Increased longevity enables millions to spend many more years with their grandchildren than ever before. Styles of grandparenting range from the remote to the highly involved with grandchildren. Jewish grandparents face problems in intergenerational contacts. Especially difficult is the question of Jewish identity of grandchildren raised in intermarried families. Grandparents are seen as vital links between past and future, and as strong role models for their grandchildren.

279. Isaacs, L. W. (1986). With our young and with our old. The Journal of Aging and Judaism, 1(1):57-67.

Attitudes of children toward the aged were studied to learn about ageism, prejudice and stereotypes. Two types of measures were employed, a social attitude scale, and six indicators of children's interaction with the aged. The sample consisted of 144

mothers, interviewed by telephone, who provided data on the frequency of their children's encounters with aged individuals, the
types of activities in which they engaged together, and the roles
of each during those contacts. Results indicated that the frequency of contact, the proximity of the residence of the old person to the child's home, the role of the old person, and the types
of activities correlated significantly with the attitudinal and
behavioral measures. The less stereotypical attitude toward the
old person was a result of collaboration between the older person
and the child. Implications of these findings for Jewish education of the children are offered.

280. Kanouse-Roberts, A. L. A study of the interaction between a
group of Jewish senior citizens and a group of Black adolescent
girls classified as delinquent. Doctoral dissertation, Columbia
University Teachers College, 1977. Dissertation Abstracts International, 38(7-A):3892.

This study was designed to explore helpful methods for over-
coming the negative effects of being known as deviants by fearful
old people. It was anticipated that social activities in a
friendly safe setting would be possible in spite of age, race and
ethnic differences of the two groups. Methodology employed included face-to-face interactions on a daily basis for three
months. This method enabled both groups to be less fearful of
each other and more tolerant and more aware of their own and other
people's feelings and behavior. Implications for education of
both young and old are offerd.

281. Roseman, Y. and Rosen, G. (Eds.) (1984). Jewish grandparent-
ing and the intergenerational connection. Summary of Proceedings.
The American Jewish Committee, Institute of Human Relations, New
York.

This report documents a scholarly conference on the importance
of Jewish grandparents as links to the past and as factors in the
identity formation of their grandchildren. Increased longevity had
made grandparenting a mass experience, rather than a privilege of
the few. Presentations include topics such as the Jewish tradition
and contemporary reality, in which there is a need to revive the
respect and the recognition for the old in general, and for the
grandparent in particular; strengthening the "vital connection,"
and looking upon the family as a source of strength and as a
healthy basis for the bond between young and old, and programming
for the intergenerational families. Recommendations on how to
achieve these goals are elaborated.

282. Schram, P. (1988).   Storytelling: A practical approach to life review. The Journal of Aging and Judaism, 2(3):188-190.

Activating all five senses, and helping older adults to recall stories of their past life are important elements of the life review process. Stories should center on places, people, objects and photographs, proverbs, folk sayings, advice, experience, diaries, letters, ethical wills, and any other personally significant recollections. Storytelling has therapeutic value for the old person. It brings to life events that were lived, recreates traditions, and enables the young to share in the old person's feelings, ideas and memories. Wisdom in the Torah is associated with the heart, not with the mind. Storytelling therefore must be directed to the heart of the listener.

283. Streltzer, A. (1979).   A grandchildren's group in a home for the aged. Health and Social Work, 4(1):168-183.

This article describes a short-term group process with young people who came regularly to the Jewish Home for the Aged in Toledo, Ohio to visit their grandparents. Grandchildren were seen by the social workers there as important links between the generations for maintaining family values, traditions, and commitments, and as valuable supports for their grandparents. The grandchildren were organized in a group so that they could gain insight into the behaviors of their parents and grandparents. A comfortable atmosphere was created in the group which fostered trust and knowledge about older people and about the services provided by the home. The quality of interaction between the generations were enhanced through this intervention, and the extended family as a whole was strengthened. Social workers are urged to look upon the family of three and four generations as the unit of treatment and upon the grandchildren as viable partners in enhancing the quality of life of aged residents in nursing homes.

Additional Resources on Jewish Aging and Aged—Not Annotated

Association for the Planning and Development of Services for the Aged in Israel, 10 Shlom Zion Hamalka, Jerusalem, Israel. Publishes annual reports on its activities (in English and Hebrew).

Bendel, J. P. and King, Y. (1984). A model for community age-integrated living for the elderly: Does it work. Jerusalem: Israel Brookdale Institute of Gerontology and Adult Human Development in Israel. "Discussion paper."

Bergman, S. (1979). A cross-national perspective on gerontology. Lectures by Simon Bergman. Denton, Center for Studies in Aging, North Texas State University.

Bergman, S. Aged in Israel, a selected bibliography. Israel Gerontological Society. P.O.B. 11243 Tel Aviv, Vol. I, 1966, Vol. II, 1976.

Breslow, Ruth W. and Van Dyk, M. (1978). Developing group homes for older people: A handbook for community groups. Jewish Council for the Aging of Greater Washington, Rockville, MD.

Brookdale Institute of Gerontology and Adult Human Development, P. O. Box 13087, Givat Ram, Jerusalem, Israel.

Cottle, T. J. (1980). Hidden survivors: Portraits of poor Jews in America. Englewood Cliffs, NJ: Prentice Hall, 1 Gulf and Western Plaza, New York, NY 10023.

Directory of Jewish homes for the aged in United States and Canada, Dallas. National Association of Jewish Homes for the Aged.

Edelman, Lily (1976). Life cycle: Programming for adults; the younger years, the buffer years, the older years; a manual and guide. Washington, D.C., B'nai B'rith.

Edelson, J. S. and Lyons, W. H. (1985). Institutional care of the
    mentally impaired elderly. Baycrest Centre for Geriatric
    Care. New York, NY: Van Nostrand Reinhold, 115 Fifth Ave-
    nue, New York, NY 10003.

Flesner, D. E. and Freed, E. D. (Eds.) (1980). Aging and the
    aged: Problems, opportunities, challenges.   Gettysburg
    College, Senior Scholars Seminar, 1979-80. Lanham, MD:
    University Press of America, 4720 Boston Way, Lanham, MD
    20706.

Hazan, H. (1980). The limbo people: A study of the constitution
    of the time universe among the aged. London; Boston; Rout-
    ledge and K. Paul.

Hendricks, J. (Ed.) (1980). In the country of the old. Farming-
    dale, NY: Baywood Publishing Co., 26 Austin, Amityville, NY
    11701.

Interdisciplinary Educational Conference on Bereavement and Grief
    (7th: 1981, New York, NY). Suicide: The will to live vs.
    the will to die. Ed. by Norman Linzer, New York: Human
    Sciences Press, 72 Fifth Avenue, New York, NY 10011.

Kaminsky, M. (1982). Daily bread, poems by Marc Kaminsky; photo-
    graphs by Leon Supraner, Urbana: University of Illinois
    Press, 54 E. Gregory Drive, Champaign, IL 61820.

Kane, R. L. and Kane. R. A. (1977). Long-term care in six coun-
    tries: Implications for the United States.   Washington,
    National Institutes of Health. DHEW Publication No. (NIH)
    76-1207.

Kramer, R. M. (1981). Voluntary agencies in the welfare state.
    Berkeley: University of California Press, 2120 Berkeley Way,
    Berkeley, CA 94720.

Kramer, S. and Masure J. (1976). Jewish grandmothers. Boston:
    Beacon Press, 25 Beacon St., Boston, MA 02108. Contents:
    Introduction, breaking stereotypes - Why they came to Ameri-
    ca? How they came, the passage to America. How they fared.

Kugelmass, J. (1986). The miracle of Intervale Avenue: The story
    of a Jewish congregation in the South Bronx. New York:
    Schocken Books, 62 Cooper Square, New York, NY 10003.

Myerhoff, B. (1978). Number our days. New York: E. P. Dutton, 2
    Park Avenue, New York, NY 10016.

Proceedings of the Seventh Annual Interdisciplinary Educational Conference on Bereavement and Grief cosponsored by Yeshiva University, the Jewish Funeral Directors of America, Inc. and allied professions, April 14, 1981.

Rosenfeld, Y. and Taske, E. (1979).   Crown Heights Jewish Community Council. Relocation of aged population from areas in decline.

Rosenthal, C. J. (1986).   Intergenerational solidarity in later life, ethnic contrasts in Jewish and Anglo families. Toronto, Ont.: Programme in Gerontology, University of Toronto.

Rubin, G., Dorff, E. N. and Bayme, S. (1986). The poor among us: Jewish tradition and social policy. New York, NY: American Jewish Committee, Institute of Human Relations, 165 W. 62nd St..

Shanan, J. (1985). Personality types and culture in later adulthood. Basel, New York: Karger. Description and analysis of the Jerusalem study of Middle Age and Aging.

Sheppard, H. L. and Kosberg, J. I. (July, 1985). The elderly in the aging society: Emerging roles and responsibilities. Presented at Symposium on Aging in the Jewish World, Jerusalem.

Silverman, P. R. (1976). If you will lift the load, I will lift it too. A guide to the creation of a widowed to widowed service. The Jewish Funeral Directors of America.

Sloan, B. (1980). The best friend you'll ever have. New York: Crown Publishers, 225 Park Avenue, S., New York, NY 10003.

Sobal, H. L. (1980). Grandpa, a young man grown old. Photographs by Patricia Agre. New York, Coward, McCann and Geog Legan, 200 Madison Avenue, New York, NY 10016.

Synagogue Council of America. That thy days may be long in the good land: A guide to aging programs for synagogues. (New York), 1975.

The Jewish aging. National Jewish population survey: Facts for planning. New York, Council of Jewish Federations, 1973.

Van Dyk, M. and Breslow, R. W. (1978). Evaluation of the Jewish Council for Aging Group Home Program. Jewish Council for the Aging of Greater Washington, Rockville, MD.

Bibliography on Aging in the Jewish World

The following articles, reports, etc. were selected from the Bibliography on Aging in the Jewish World, published by the JDC-Brookdale Institute of Gerontology and Adult Human Development, Jerusalem, in cooperation with JDC-Israel and the International Coordinating Council on Aging in the Jewish World. They are presented here as additional helpful resource material.

General

Bergman, S. (1985). "Israel-Diaspora Relations on Aging". Aging in the Jewish World Series, AJW-3. Brookdale Institute of Gerontology, Jerusalem.

Katan, J. and Spiro, S. (1985). "Participation of the Aged." Aging in the Jewish World Series, AJW-17. Brookdale Institute of Gerontology, Jerusalem.

Kremsdorf, E. (1985). "Early Retirement–– A Challenge for the Communities? Aging in the Jewish World Series, AJW-24. Brookdale Institute of Gerontology, Jerusalem.

Morris, R. (1985). "Social Implications of an Aging Society: Vigor, Disability and Dependency in Mature Societies". Aging in the Jewish World Series, AJW-7. Brookdale Institute of Gerontology, Jerusalem.

Sheppard, H. and Kosberg, J. (1985). "The Elderly in an Aging Society: Emerging Roles and Responsibilities". Aging in the Jewish World Series, AJW-2. Brookdale Institute of Gerontology, Jerusalem.

Warach, B. (1985). "The Status of the Jewish Elderly in the United States." Aging in the Jewish World Series, AJW-49. Brookdale Institute of Gerontology, Jerusalem.

Warach, B. (1981). "The Aged —Introduction", in The Turbulent Decades: Jewish Communal Services in America 195878 Volume I. Conference of Jewish Communal Services, New York.

Wolfe, C. (1985). "Sharing Information in the Jewish World Aging Network." Aging in the Jewish World Series, AJW19. Brookdale Institute of Gerontology, Jerusalem.

Yeshiva University Gerontological Institute and the Wurzweiler School of Social Work (1984). Honor Thy Father and Thy Mother: Perspectives on Filial Responsibility.

Planning Documents

Communal Planning Committee on Aging—New York (1984). The Communal Planning Committee on Aging: The Five Year Plan for Services to the Aged.

Fuld, J. (1985). "Jewish Communal Planning of Services for the Elderly in Small Jewish Communities". Aging in the Jewish World Series, AJW-12. Brookdale Institute of Gerontology, Jerusalem.

Jewish Convalescent Hospital, Social Work Department (1984). Report to the Task Force on Services to the Elderly. Jewish Family Services Social Service Center, Montreal.

Laor, U. (1985). "Assisting the Development of Local Services for the Elderly: The Experience of Israel". Aging in the Jewish World Series, AJW-23. Brookdale Institute of Gerontology, Jerusalem.

Sainer, J. and Mayer, M. (1985). "Approaches to Planning and Priority Setting for the Jewish Community". Aging in the Jewish World Series, AJW-20. Brookdale Institute of Gerontology, Jerusalem.

Weismehl, R. (1985). "Planning and Implementing a Community Care Program for the Elderly: A Sharing of Practice Wisdom". Aging in the Jewish World Series, AJW-1. Brookdale Institute of Gerontology, Jerusalem.

Service Provision and Evaluation

Carlowe, M. (1985). "New and Emerging Patterns within Jewish Communal Services for the Frail and Elderly". Aging in the Jewish World Series, AJW-5. Brookdale Institute of Gerontology, Jerusalem.

Council of Jewish Federations—New York (1982). Innovative Services for the Elderly: A Program Information Exchange.

Dorman, S. (1984). Report on Senior Citizens' Community Project. Cape Jewish Welfare Council, Cape Town, South Africa.

Eran, Y. (1979). "Innovations in Services for the Aged in Israel" in Teicher, M.; Thurz, D. and Vigilante, J. (eds.), Reaching the Aged. Sage Publications, Beverly Hills, pp. 31-42.

Gottesman, L. and Cohen, E. (1985). "Meeting the Challenge of the Rapid Increase in the Needs of the Elderly". Aging in the Jewish World Series, AJW-2. Brookdale Institute of Gerontology, Jerusalem.

Hassan, J. (1985). "Challenge of the Rapid Increase in the Needs of the Disabled Elderly". Aging in the Jewish World Series, AJW-39. Brookdale Institute of Gerontology, Jerusalem.

Isaacs, B. (1985). "Providing Health Care and Maintaining Health". Aging in the Jewish World Series, AJW-2. Brookdale Institute of Gerontology, Jerusalem.

Jackson, A. and Borth, L. (1983). Alternatives in Living Arrangements for the Elderly. Volume 2. Conference on Shared Living, convened by Jewish Center for Aged, St. Louis, Missouri in cooperation with Council of Jewish Federations, New York.

Jewish Child and Family Service—Winnipeg (1984). A Subsidized Taxi Service for the Winnipeg Jewish Elderly.

Jewish Community Council of Ottawa (1982). Report of the Sub-Panel on Services to the Jewish Elderly.

Jewish Nursing Home—Montreal (1984). Jewish Home Care Services. Report to Council on Aging of Allied Jewish Community Services, Montreal.

Joint Jewish Community Council of Ottawa, Jewish Home for the Aged Task Force (1982). Future Directions for Hillel Lodge.

Kahana, E. and Kahana, B. (1983). Jewish Elderly in the United States. Elderly Care Research Center, Cleveland, Ohio.

Kargan, M. (1986). Jewish Ethnicity and Home Support Care—Seminar Proceedings, June 1986. Sydney Jewish Centre on Aging, Woollahra.

Lerba, C. (1985). "A Locally-Based Community Center for Jewish Aging: Concepts in Practice". Aging in the Jewish World Series, AJW-29. Brookdale Institute of Gerontology, Jerusalem.

Lippman, W. and Borowski, A. (1985). "Aging in the Australian Jewish Community". Aging in the Jewish World Series, AJW-8. Brookdale Institute of Gerontology, Jerusalem.

Litwin, H. (1985). "Community Centers and the Elderly: An American and Israeli Comparison". Aging in the Jewish World Series, AJW-40. Brookdale Institute of Gerontology, Jerusalem.

Novick, L. (1985). "Meeting the Needs of the Jewish Elderly in Canada". Aging in the Jewish World Series, AJW-11 and AJW-4 (summary version). Brookdale Institute of Gerontology, Jerusalem.

Shore, H. (1983). Alternative Living Arrangements for the Elderly. Council of Jewish Federations, New York.

Social/Cultural Aspects

Hantman, S. (1985). "The Family and the Elderly in a Changing Society." Aging in the Jewish World Series, AJW-31. Brookdale Institute of Gerontology, Jerusalem.

Handlin, M.; Layton, E.; Smith, M.; and Casserd, R. (1983). Let Me Hear Your Voice: Portraits of Aging Immigrant Jews. University of Washington, Seattle.

Heschel, A. (1981). "The Older Person and the Family in the Perspective of the Jewish Tradition," in Le Fevre, C. and L. (eds.), Aging and the Human Spirit. Exploration Press, Chicago.

Kahana, B. and Kahana, E. (1985). "Jewish Aged and Their Families Cross-National Perspectives". Aging in the Jewish World Series, AJW-25. Brookdale Institute of Gerontology, Jerusalem.

Lamm, M. (1983). Jewish Perspectives on Death and Dying. Council of Jewish Federations, New York.

Myerhoff, B. (1978). "A Symbol Perfected in Death: Continuity and Ritual in the Life and Death of an Elderly Jew",
in B. Myerhoff and A. Simic, Life's Career--Aging:
Cultural Variations on Growing Old. Sage Publications,
Beverly Hills.

Schwartz, A. (1985). "Identity, Community and Aging". Aging
in the Jewish World Series, AJW-31. Brookdale Institute
of Gerontology, Jerusalem.

Selzer, S. (ed.) (1979). So Teach Us to Number Our Days: A
Manual on Aging for Synagogue Use. New York, The Union
of American Hebrew Congregations.

Weisman, C. (1985). "The Needs of the Jewish Elderly:
What's Happened to Spirituality"? Aging in the Jewish
World Series, AJW-16. Brookdale Institute of Geron-
tology, Jerusalem.

Needs Assessment/Local Population Surveys

Federation of Jewish Agencies of Greater Philadelphia (1984).
The Jewish Population of the Greater Philadelphia Area.
Report by W. Yancey and I. Goldstein. Philadelphia
Institute for Public Policy Studies, Social Science Data
Library, Temple University.

Federation of Jewish Philanthropies--New York (1985). The
Jewish Population of Greater New York: Profiles of
Counties, Boroughs, and Areas.

Habib, J. (1987). "Survey of Aging in the Jewish World:
Highlights". Aging in the Jewish World Series, AJW-45.
Brookdale Institute of Gerontology, Jerusalem.

Habib, J. (1987). "Survey of Aging in the Jewish World:
Worldwide Report". Aging in the Jewish World Series,
AJW-43. Brookdale Institute of Gerontology, Jerusalem.

Jewish Community Federation--Richmond, Virginia (1984).
Demographic Survey of the Jewish Community of Richmond.

Jewish Federation of Pittsburgh (1984). Demographic Survey
of Pittsburgh: 1984.

Jewish Federation of St. Louis (1985). Analysis of Population Aged 50 Years and Older". Report to the Long-Range Planning Committee for the Elderly.

Jewish Welfare Federation of Detroit (1984). The Jewish Elderly of Metropolitan Detroit: A Socio-Demographic and Needs Assessment Study. Conducted by the University of Michigan.

Jimack, M. (1983). Jewish Senior Citizens in South London: A Study of Social and Community Needs. Central Council for Jewish Social Service, London.

Kantrowitz, S. (1980). Demographic Study of Jewish Aged. Montreal.

Kargan, M. (1986). Demography, Health and Lifestyles: Sydney Old-Old Jews. Report of 1984 Survey. Sydney Jewish Centre on Aging, Woollahra.

Phillips, B. and Weinberg, E. (1984). The Milwaukee Jewish Population: Report of a Survey. Prepared for the Milwaukee Jewish Federation, Inc. Policy Research Corporation, Chicago, Illinois.

Sheskin, I. (1984). Summary Report: A Demographic Study of the Greater Miami Jewish Community. Report to the Greater Miami Jewish Federation, Miami, Florida.

"Survey Shows Greater Boston Jewry on Rise" (1986). The Jewish Advocate, March 27.

Tobin, G. (1984). A Demographic Study of the Jewish Community of Greater Washington, 1983. Center for Modern Jewish Studies, Brandeis University, Waltham, Massachusetts. Prepared for the United Jewish Appeal Federation of Greater Washington, Inc. Bethesda, Maryland.

Demography

Della Pergola, S. (1985). "Some Demographic, Socio-Economic and Jewish Identity Characteristics of the Jewish Elderly: A Cross-National Profile, 1965-1976". Aging in the Jewish World Series, AJW-10. Brookdale Institute of Gerontology, Jerusalem.

Goldschmidt, N. (1985). "A Brief Guide to Official Statistics on the Elderly Population of Israel". Aging in the Jewish World Series, AJW-14. Brookdale Institute of Gerontology, Jerusalem.

Goldstein, S. (1983). Review of Jewish Population Studies in the United States of America, 1972-1979. Jewish Population Studies Series. The Institute of Contemporary Jewry, The Hebrew University of Jerusalem and the Institute of Jewish Affairs, London.

Huberman, S. (1984). Using Jewish Population Study Data for Decision-making: Theoretical Considerations and Practice Experience. Perspectives in Jewish Population Research. Waltham Center for Modern Jewish Studies and Westview Press, Denver.

Schmelz, U. (1985). "The Aging of World Jewry: A Summary". Aging in the Jewish World Series, AJW-9. Brookdale Institute of Gerontology, Jerusalem.

Schmelz, U.; Glikson, P.; and DellaPergola, S. (eds.) (1983, 1980, 1977). Papers in Jewish Demography, 1981, 1977, 1973. Institute of Contemporary Jewry, in cooperation with the World Union of Jewish Studies and the Association for Jewish Demography and Statistics, Jerusalem.

Statistics Canada (1981). Census. Vol. 1-National Series on Population; Vol. 2-Provincial Series: 93-925-93-934: Language, ethnic origin, religion, place of birth, schooling for all provinces; Vol. 3- Profile Series B. 95-941. Federal electoral district-selected social and economic characteristics. (Included for reportage on Jewish community)

Service Directories

National Association of Homes for the Aged (1983). Directory of Jewish Homes for the Aged in the United States and Canada, 1982-1983.

Robbins, I. (1985). North American Association of Jewish Homes and Housing for the Aging: Directory, Dallas.

Wolf, D. (1983). Innovative Services for the Elderly: Programs Sponsored by the Federation of Jewish Philanthropies of New York and the Agencies. Council of Jewish Federations, New York.

Questionnaires[1]

Bergman, S.; Holmes, D.; and Holmes, M. (1984). Study: Informal Support of Elderly in Kibbutzim. Instruments: (1) Kibbutz Case Study Interview; (2) Older Person Screening Interview; (3) Older Person Extended Interview; and (4) Caregiver Interview Schedule, Brookdale Institute-Jerusalem and Community Research Associates--New York. (Hebrew and English)

Brookdale Institute and Jerusalem Municipality (1978). Study: Community Study of Life Patterns. Social and Medical Needs and Services. Instruments Survey Questionnaire for the Elderly. Jerusalem (Hebrew and English)

Davies, M. (1987). Study: Epidemiology of Senile Dementia. Instruments: Quick Screening Survey Instrument for Elderly in the Community. Brookdale Institute--Jerusalem. (French, Hebrew, English, Russian, Yiddish, Romanian, Spanish and Arabic)

Factor, H. and Shmueli, A. (1984). Study: Appropriateness of Care for Elderly Receiving Services in the Community and for Elderly Awaiting Institutionalization. Instruments: (1) Client Questionnaire; (2) Professional Caregiver Questionnaire; (3) Informal Caregiver Questionnaire; (4) Informal Caregiver in Lieu of Client Questionnaire. Brookdale Institute, Jerusalem (Hebrew and English)

Fleishman, R. (1984). Study: Quality of Care in the Burzaco Old Age Home (Buenos Aires, Argentina). Instruments for a Concise Evaluation of an Old Age Home. Instruments: (1) Questionnaire for Residents; (2) Questionnaire for Head Physician; (3) Questionnaire for Head Social Worker; (4) Questionnaire for Head Nurse; (5) Questionnaire for Administrative Director; (6) Questionnaire for Home Professionals. Brookdale Institute, Jerusalem (English and Spanish)

---

[1]A collection of questionnaires used in Jewish community surveys is also available from the North American Jewish Data Bank, Center for Jewish Studies, Box 465, 33 West 42 Street, New York, N.Y. 10036, USA.

Fleishman, R.; Tomer, A. et al. (1986). Study: Evaluation of Quality of Care in Long-Term Care Institutions in Israel: The Tracer Approach. Instruments: (1) Measurement of the Quality of Care in Long-Term Care in Israel. Instruments, and (2) Recommended Instruments for Measuring the Quality of Long-Term Care. Brookdale Institute, Jerusalem (Hebrew and English)

Habib, J. and M. Korazhim (1985). Study: Aging in the Jewish World: An International Study on Jewish Community Programming for the Elderly. Instruments Questionnaire on Service Provision, Demography, Service Planning, Evaluation and Manpower. Brookdale Institute, Jerusalem (English, Spanish and French)

Heuman, L. (1986). Study: Management of Sheltered Housing for the Elderly. Instruments: (1) Sheltered Housing Questionnaire for Housemothers (Site Managers) and (2) Sheltered Housing Questionnaire for Community Service Coordinators. Brookdale Institute, Jerusalem (Hebrew and English)

Jewish Community Council of Dayton, Ohio (1979). Study: Community Aged Study. Instruments: Survey of Needs of Jewish Older People (on Housing, Health, Social Relationships, Transportation, Employment). Jewish Community Council of Greater Dayton Coordinating Committee on Services to the Aged—Dayton, Ohio.

Jimack, M. (1985). Study: Jewish Senior Citizens in South London: Study of Social and Community Needs. Instruments: South London Survey: Questionnaire for Persons Over 60 Years (on Housing, Health, Social Service Needs and Attitudes to Voluntarism). Central Council for Jewish Social Service — London.

Kahana, B.; Harel, Z.; and Kahana, E. (1983). Study: Oakland University Holocaust Studies Project. Instruments: Holocaust, Survivors Interview (Hebrew and English)

Kahana, E. and Kahana, B. (1978). Study: Voluntary Relocation and Adaptation of the Aged. Instruments: (1) Pre-Israel Questionnaire and (2) Post-Israel Questionnaire. Elderly Care Research Center. Wayne State University, Detroit (Hebrew and English)

Litwin, H. and Budkowski, D. (1984). Study: Evaluation of Programs for the Elderly in Community Centers. Instruments: Questionnaire for Community Center Directors. Brookdale Institute, Jerusalem (Hebrew and English)

Appendix: Related Journals

The journals listed below can help users of this bibliography to keep their readings current.

Activities, Adaptation and Aging; the journal of active management.
>   Haworth Press, Inc.
>   12 W. 32nd Street
>   New York, NY 10001

Administration in Social Work; the quarterly journal of human services management.
>   Haworth Press, Inc.
>   12 W. 32nd Street
>   New York, NY 10001

Ageing International; text in English and Spanish.
>   1909 K Street, NW
>   Washington, DC 20049

Ageing and Society
>   Cambridge University Press
>   32 E. 57th Street
>   New York, NY 10022

Aging
>   Administration on Aging
>   U.S. Office of Human Development
>   U.S. Department of Health and Human Services
>   Washington, DC 20201

American Jewish Committee
>   165 E. 65th Street
>   New York, NY 10022

American Jewish Historical Quarterly
    Two Thornton Road
    Waltham, MA 02154

American Journal of Orthopsychiatry
    19 W. 44th Street
    New York, NY 10036

American Quarterly
    309 College Hall
    University of Pennsylvania
    Philadelphia, PA 19104-6303

American Journal of Social Psychiatry
    1400 K Street, NW
    Washington, DC 20005

Archiv Fuer Psychologie; text in English and German.
    Postfach 1268
    D-5300 Bonn, W. Germany

Current Anthropology; world journal of the sciences of
man.
    University of Chicago Press
    5801 S. Ellis Avenue
    Chicago, IL 60637

Educational Gerontology; an international bi monthly
journal.
    Hemisphere Publishing Corporation
    1010 Vermont Avenue, NW
    Washington, DC 20005

Ethnicity
    Academic Press
    111 5th Avenue
    New York, NY 10003

Generations; the spiritual enrichment newsletter for
mature Catholics.
    Claretian Publications
    205 W. Monroe Street
    Chicago, IL 60606

Gerontologist, The
    Gerontological Society of America
    1411 K Street, NW
    Ste. 300
    Washington, DC 20005

Gerontology and Geriatric Education
> Haworth Press, Inc.
> 12 W. 32nd Street
> New York, NY 10001

Human Organization
> Society for Applied Anthropology
> Box 24083
> Oklahoma City, OK 73124-0084

International Forum for Logotherapy; the search for
meaning.
> Institute for Logotherapy
> 2000 Dwight Way
> Berkeley, CA 94704

International Journal of Aging and Human Development
> Baywood Publishing Company, Inc.
> 120 Marine Street
> Box D
> Farmingdale, NY 11735

International Journal of Nursing Studies; text in
English, French, Russian, Spanish.
> Pergamon Press, Inc.
> Journals Division
> Maxwell House
> Fairview Park, Elmsford, NY 10523

**International Journal of Offender Therapy and
Comparative Criminology**
> Oregon Health Sciences University
> Department of Psychiatry
> 114 Gaines Hall
> 840 S. W. Gaines Road
> Portland, OR 97201

International Journal of Social Psychiatry
> Avenue Publishing Co.
> 55 Woodstock Avenue
> London NW11 9RG, England

International Journal of the Sociology of Language; an
interdisciplinary journal of the language sciences
(text in English, French, German).
> 200 Saw Mill River Road
> Hawthorne New York, NY 10532

Israel Annals of Psychiatry and Related Disciplines
Jerusalem Academic Press
Box 3640
Jerusalem, Israel

Israel Journal of Medical Sciences; text in English.
Israel Journal of Medical Sciences
P. O. B. 1435
Jerusalem 91013, Israel.

Issues in Mental Health Nursing
Hemisphere Publishing Corporation
79 Madison Avenue
New York, NY 10016

Jewish Journal of Sociology
187 Gloucester Place
London NW1 6BU, England

Jewish Social Studies; text in English.
Centre for Social Studies
University of Dacca
Arts Building
Dacca 2, Bangladesh

Journal of Advanced Nursing
Blackwell Scientific Publications Ltd.
Osney Mead
Oxford OX 2 OEL, England

Journal of Aging and Judaism
Human Science Press
72 Fifth Avenue
New York, NY 10011

Journal of Cross-Cultural Gerontology
Reidel Publishing Co.
Box 17
3300 AD Dordrecht, Netherlands

Journal of Ethnic Studies
Western Washington University
Bellingham, WA 98225

Journal of Geriatric Psychiatry
International Universities Press Inc.
Journal Department
59 Boston Post Road
Box 1524
Madison, CT 06443-1524

Journal of Gerontological Nursing
Sack Inc.
6900 Grove Road
Thorofare, NJ 08086

Journal of Gerontological Social Work
Haworth Press, Inc.
12 W. 32nd Street
New York, NY 10001

Journal of Gerontology
Gerontological Society of America
1411 K Street, NW
Ste. 300
Washington, DC 20005

Journal of Jewish Communal Service
Conference of Jewish Communal Services
15 E. 26th Street
New York, NY 10010

Journal of Marriage and the Family
National Council of Family Relations
1910 W. County Road B
Ste. 147
St. Paul, MN 55113

Journal of Nutrition for the Elderly
Haworth Press, Inc.
12 W. 32nd Street
New York, NY 10001

Journal of Occupational Psychology
British Psychological Society
St. Andrews House
48 Princess Road E.
Leicester LE1 7DR, England

Journal of Psychology and Judaism
Human Sciences Press, Inc.
72 Fifth Avenue
New York, NY 10011

Journal of Religion and Aging
Haworth Press, Inc.
12 W. 32nd Street
New York, NY 10001

Journal of Social Issues
    Plenum Press
    233 Spring Street
    New York, NY 10013

Journal of Social Work and Policy in Israel
    Bar-Ilan University Press
    Bar-Ilan University
    Ramat Gan, Israel

Journal of Sociology and Social Welfare
    University of Connecticut
    School of Social Work
    1800 Asylum Avenue
    W. Hartford, CT 06117

Journal of the American Geriatrics Society
    Elsevier Science Publishing, Co.
    52 Vanderbilt Avenue
    New York, NY 10017

Journal of Urban History
    Sage Publications, Inc.
    2111 W. Hillcrest Drive
    Newbury Park, CA 91320

Journal of Vocational Behavior
    Academic Press, Inc.
    Journal Division
    1250 Sixth Avenue
    San Diego, CA 92101

Maryland State Medical Journal
    Medical and Chirurgical Faculty to the State of
    Maryland
    1211 Cathedral Street
    Baltimore, MD 21201

Medical Education
    Blackwell Scientific Publications, Ltd.
    Osney Mead
    Oxford OX2 OEL, England

Moment
    Jewish Educational Ventures, Inc.
    462 Boylston Street
    Boston, MA 02116

New York Council of Jewish Federation and Welfare Funds
Council of Jewish Federations, Inc.
Endowment Development Department
730 Broadway
New York, NY 10003

New York History
New York State Historical Association
Box 800
Cooperstown, NY 13326

Population and Environment; Behavioral and Social Issues
Human Sciences Press, Inc.
72 Fifth Avenue
New York, NY 10011

Present Tense; the magazine of world Jewish affairs.
American Jewish Committee
165 East 56 Street
New York, NY 10022

Reconstructionist
Federation of Reconstructionist Congregations and
Havurot
270 West 89th Street
New York, NY 10024

Religious Education; a platform for the free discussion
of issues in the field of religion and their bearing
on education.
Religious Education Association
409 Prospect Street
New Haven, CT 06511

Research on Aging; a quarterly of social gerontology and
adult development.
Sage Publications, Inc.
211 W. Hillcrest Dr.
Newbury Park, CA 91320

Social Casework; the journal of contemporary social
work.
Family Service of America
11700 W. Lake Park Drive
Milwaukee, WI 53224

Social Science and Medicine
Pergamon Press, Inc.
Journals Division
Maxwell House
Fairview Park
Elmsford, NY 10523

Social Work
   National Association of Social Workers
   Publications Department
   7981 Eastern Avenue
   Silver Spring, MD 20910

Social Work in Health Care; quarterly journal of medical
   and psychiatric social work.
   Haworth Press, Inc.
   12 W. 32nd Street
   New York, NY 10001

Social Work Papers
   Houston, Texas (University)
   Ohio State University
   University of Southern California

Tradition: A Journal of Orthodox Thoughts
   Rabbinical Council of America
   275 7th Avenue
   New York, NY   10001

Author Index

Note: References below are to entry, not page numbers.

Subject Index

Note: References below are to entry, not page numbers.

About the Compiler

DAVID GUTTMANN is Dean and Associate Professor in the School of Social Work, the University of Haifa, Israel. His previous works include *European-American Elderly: A Guide for Practice, European-American Elderly: An Annotated Bibliography,* and articles published in *Social Thought,* the *Journal of Cross Cultural Gerontology, The Gerontologist, Human Development American Rehabilitation,* and *Generations.*